TOPIC TEACHING IN THE PRIMARY SCHOOL

Topic Teaching in the Primary School

TEACHING ABOUT SOCIETY THROUGH TOPIC WORK

STELLA GUNNING, DENNIS GUNNING
AND JACK WILSON

ROUTLEDGE

First published 1981 by Croom Helm Ltd
Reprinted by Routledge 1990
11 New Fetter Lane, London EC4P 4EE

© 1981 Stella Gunning, Dennis Gunning and Jack Wilson

Typeset by Jayell Typesetting - London
Printed and bound in Great Britain
by Billing and Sons Limited, Worcester

British Library Cataloguing in Publication Data

Gunning, Stella
    Topic teaching in the primary school.
    1. Social sciences – Study and teaching
    (Elementary)
    I. Title II. Gunning, Dennis III. Wilson, Jack
    372.8'3   LB1584
    ISBN 0-415-05152-5

CONTENTS

ACKNOWLEDGEMENTS

Pictures courtesy of: Macdonald Educational, pp. 55, 56; Macmillan Educational, p. 57; Longmans Ltd, p. 60; Faber and Faber, p. 129; The Trustees of the British Museum, p. 193; Blackwells Ltd, p. 196.

INTRODUCTION

Primary school teachers are expected to cope with the whole of a school's curriculum and to teach almost a full programme of all types of work from music to science. When they have to deal with lively, rapidly learning young minds who are stimulated outside school by a range of other experiences offered by television, holidays and social contacts, they are constantly challenged. It is difficult – no, impossible – for teachers to be equally expert in every area and to meet the expectations of professionals who are specialists in any one field. The purpose of this book is to help them to plan and teach effectively in that area of primary school work often called 'topic'. By this coverall we intend to include material derived from history, geography and social sciences. Topic work occupies anything from three to ten hours a week according to how it is defined and organised. Important though it is, busy teachers probably have to give energy and attention first of all to literacy and numeracy so, in this book, we are assuming that they do not have unlimited time or resources for 'topic' work. What are the chief worries and anxieties teachers have about topic work?

Most teachers are deeply disquieted, when they have successfully launched a new topic on say, exploration, and the children seem interested and well motivated, to find that their children who are using books to find out about, for example, Columbus, are copying from them in spite of exhortation to express themselves in their own words. They may be copying text, a map and a picture of the *Santa Maria*. Their class teacher is dubious about the value of the activity but with questions from other children, requests for help for the model-makers and the search for material for boys interested in space travel, the week may end without the problem of copying being solved. He can, however, be quite sure that it will reappear shortly in the context of the next session on topics.

Books for topic work, too, are a constant headache. There is comparatively little published for the really hesitant reader and the Macmillan series 'Starters' and 'First Library', and Blackwell's 'Little Library' are invaluable but do not cover every possible area. Many of the books apparently intended for the primary school child in this area have a vocabulary which is typical only of readers of above average level, and some are so dense in appearance as to be discouraging. And then there is the question of expense. Even with the welcome help of public libraries it is nearly impossible to provide every child in the class with suitable material on a given subject. One solution to this dilemma is to tackle topics which use children's day-to-day experience and which can be successfully carried out either without books or, in the case say of a study on 'Uniforms', with very few books. Such topics, too, which are based on and develop children's understanding of society and human behaviour, do not necessarily require the teacher to have a high level of specialist knowledge. It has been suggested that primary school children should not be learning anything which an educated adult does not already know or cannot very easily find out. In this area – social studies – we all know a great deal more than we imagine, if we ask ourselves the key questions and reflect on our experience.

All teachers agree that they should match the task set to the child's capacity. In some areas, it is immediately obvious if one has failed to do this – the child cannot do the maths task or completes it and other examples at a speed which indicates boredom. In topic work, however, the matter is more problematic. The level of difficulty relates closely to conceptual level. By a concept we mean an abstraction, like 'exploration', which gives a name to a characterised range of human activities, or 'harbour', which classifies together particular land forms with a common characteristic. In handling concepts there may be a reading difficulty – the child cannot read the word – or a difficulty of understanding – the child has never seen a picture of a harbour or visited one and consequently the term is meaningless. We will devote a lot of attention to the matter of conceptual understanding. We propose to suggest simple ways of finding out what level of conceptual understanding children have. Our experience here suggests that while teachers overestimate what secondary children understand, they probably underestimate what the conceptual development is of young age groups. In addition, we shall suggest a variety of strategies for developing conceptual understanding and enabling teachers to set tasks appropriate to the level of understanding revealed by different groups of children and different individuals. For example, it may be appropriate to say to one child, 'Find me a picture of a harbour and write a sentence about it', while for another one might say, 'Look at the large scale map and find a place which has a harbour. What makes a good harbour?'

A problem which exercises student teachers particularly is providing children with a variety of activities within topic work. They find that their lesson plans may fall into a stereotyped pattern which repeats itself in a boring way, or that all the work they suggest involves similar reading and writing activities so that the children get restless and say, 'Can't we do something else?' When they try to provide a variety, the ideas which come to mind are drawing pictures or making models. There is, however, the lurking suspicion that these are often activities neither involving learning nor achieving any level of artistic creativity or skill. In a word they are busy work, which fills the time but are difficult to justify except in terms of producing 'wall paper' as evidence of topic activity. We hope to suggest activities like, for example, making a frieze depicting a known street which may be evaluated in terms of the understanding which it shows of the subject studied.

While student teachers plan their work for comparatively short bursts of time, i.e. the length of a school practice, as soon as they get into school they have to plan over a much longer period, usually a year, and have to consider how their plan fits into the longer perspective of the child's primary school life. Critics have not been slow to point out the incoherence of much topic work, and teachers are sometimes at a loss to explain to parents why a topic on 'exploration' is followed by one on 'birds' or 'people who help us'. If teachers simply select their topics without regard to the work done by children in the previous class there is a danger of repetition, and many children have sighed as 'autumn' or 'Guy Fawkes' have come round for the fourth or fifth time. Few people have tackled in print the problem of reconciling the need for flexibility with a structural progression within primary school topic work, except for the team who produced *Social Studies 8-13*, a useful contribution to a controversial topic. The controversy arises perhaps because some teachers would insist on the primacy of children's interests as the principle of selection in determining choices of content in topic work. Others might suggest that it is not easy to decide what children's interests are. They vary from one individual to another and from one generation of children to another. There is a considerable danger of interpreting the interests of a particular group of children in terms of what have become the established conventions of topic work. We shall suggest that the interests of children may not be confined to the topics which repetition has made banal and that their experiences are more wide-ranging than often assumed.

There is a danger too that the supposed interests of children may become a confining straightjacket. Little girls are assumed to be interested in feminine and homemaking activities. It is a pity if their topic work reinforces the cultural conditioning they receive by limiting them to topics on 'costume' and activities like dressing dolls, instead of encouraging them to undertake more challenging and adventurous studies. And finally as schools are increasingly open to challenge by parents and the public there is the crunch-question — are the topics studied 'worthwhile'. We have all looked at some examples of children's work and wondered if the subject was not too trivial or banal to stimulate worthwhile reading. Some children's only interest seems to be football or pop music — does this have to consist of cutting out pictures and sticking them into a scrap book? Can subjects such as this produce the development of concepts and intellectual skills?

Teachers who were themselves raised on a diet of traditional disciplines rather than interdisciplinary or integrated studies, and who know that these disciplines still dominate the secondary school curriculum, are sometimes anxious about whether or not they should introduce their primary school pupils to subjects such as history and geography instead of using the topic approach. In this book examples will be given of teaching materials which can serve as models of straightforward discipline-based work in, for instance, history, for we really are not taking sides in a 'Topic v. Subjects' debate. Our concern is with quality of work in the social studies area, not, primarily, with how the work is organised.

Recent years have seen an increased pressure to make schools and teachers accountable to the community and for more stringent attempts to evaluate the effectiveness of teaching. This has made thoughtful teachers try to analyse exactly what can be expected of the children they teach. What, in fact, should a child leaving the primary school be able to do in the sphere of social studies? Most people would reject the idea, once more commonly found, that there is a particular body of knowledge all children should have. Teachers increasingly have argued that they teach children the skills with which to find out. Most teachers would include here the ability to use an index, a dictionary and an encyclopedia: we ourselves would stress that there is a range of intellectual skills, for example the skills of interpreting data, of giving arguments pro and con, of making judgements, and that these skills can be cultivated. We hope to show how this may be done in a variety of different ways. We therefore would hope to illuminate the nature of what children should learn to do in the primary school — for example, we would expect that children would acquire the confidence and the understanding of the nature of knowledge to be able to say, on appropriate occasions, 'I don't know the answer to x. Perhaps nobody knows it.'

While teachers would certainly claim that they intend to develop mathematical and scientific concepts, few would argue that instead of a body of knowledge they hoped to procure conceptual understanding in the area traditionally known as 'topic'. We would, however, hope to show that within this area of the curriculum children do develop social, economic and even political understanding and that this area may be justified for its contribution to the growth in children of a network of concepts, the possession of which characterises the educated mind. And we are happy to indicate a few of the concepts we consider sufficiently significant to be cultivated within the curriculum, so that practising teachers may be encouraged to formulate their own lists of key concepts worth systematic cultivation.

A particularly vexed question is the matter of the relationship between educational theory and classroom practice. Teachers are aware of the body of educational theory but many are dubious about its exact relevance to classroom practice. Their doubts are enhanced when, after many years during which Piaget was widely quoted as the dominant influence on British primary school philosophy, his work and its effects are now subject to criticism. And when they read that Bruner argues that any subject can be taught to any child of any age in an intellectually respectable form, they may well wonder what implication this claim has for their work: in what sense can — should — sociology and anthropology be taught in primary schools? While this book does not claim to be a work of educational theory we would hope to relate theory to practice within the context of topic work and to show how the work of Piaget, Bruner and others, relates to the methods we propose.

Finally, we should make our declaration of faith. In spite of the challenges offered by topic work in primary schools, we would like to stress its importance. In this area lies the means of cultivating children's understanding of not just their physical environment, the importance of which has long been appreciated in primary education, but the social and human environment in which they are growing up and which they are seeking help in interpreting. Children are interested in human behaviour, human dilemmas, human achievements, especially when these are presented in terms of the social groups in which they live, their friendships, family, school and neighbourhood groups. While the problems of nation and state may appear too complex for them, as they are for many adults, their capacity to understand the problems of day-to-day life is often underestimated and remains uncultivated. There is a gap in their education here and in this book we would like to suggest ways of filling it.

PART ONE

THE CONTEXT OF TOPIC WORK

1 THE CONTEXT OF TOPIC WORK IN THE PRIMARY SCHOOL

In this chapter we propose to look closer at the assumptions about the nature of learning which will underpin this book. Unfortunately, we are unable to cite many experiments in or statistical data on the learning process in this field, since they virtually do not exist. It is tragic that, given the large number of students of education, so few have been stimulated to work in this field and that, while in some areas such as mathematics, there is a large body of literature, you could probably read nearly all there is in print on young children's understanding and progress in the area of history, geography or social studies in an energetic weekend. It is even difficult to find in print examples of children's work in the field. Where samples of children's work is published, it is usually being held up for admiration and is only too often of such a high standard that teachers looking at it may be disheartened if not overtly sceptical. Certainly we can think of no printed examples of children's work where the purpose is to examine failures in teaching or learning and to consider what action might be taken to remedy the situation.

If this sounds a very gloomy beginning let us hasten to say that there is a body of theoretical writing, largely that of Piaget and Bruner, which, while it is not overtly concerned with primary school topic work or social studies or the disciplines which contribute to both, has sometimes influenced teachers' practices and assumptions, those who have tried to reform the primary school curriculum, or those launching innovations in curricular practice. Both these psychologists have interested themselves in the young child's learning processes, considered in relation to the content of the curriculum – in the case of Piaget chiefly in mathematics and science, and in the case of Bruner on a broader front, including social organisation. Here it is enough to say that they, together with other educational psychologists, are convinced of the central importance of conceptual development in the process of intellectual growth. There is also evidence to suggest that children's success in school subjects depends substantially on their conceptual development and that it is not enough to leave conceptual development to chance.

You may say at this point, 'But hasn't Piaget shown that intellectual development is dependent on maturation? If it is related to children's physical growth how can it be hurried?' It is true that in the small groups of children Piaget used for his major mathematical investigations, he found a relationship between age and progress to what he calls 'concrete operations' at the age of seven or eight and to 'formal operations' at adolescence. He added however that such progress takes place in a rich educational environment. He did not expect that his work would be used to justify an educational philosophy of non-intervention and did not intend to advocate such a policy. Recently his work has come under criticism on a number of counts: for example, the size of the group of children he studied was very small. It has been claimed too that if children are given intelligent instruction, the results of the experiments are modified. It is not however the work of Piaget, but the interpretation of it in British schools which has been very fiercely attacked by Professor Vincent Rogers. This American authority deplores the effects of Piaget's influence on British primary school social studies which he claims results in 'overly simplistic, intellectually undemanding studies emphasising the concrete and therefore the nearby while consistently putting off more challenging approaches which might begin to develop more complex thinking strategies . . . at much earlier age levels'. In other words, because British teachers have come to believe that it may be harmful to give children instruction before they are ready for it they have tended to underestimate what, given skilful teaching, young children can do in this area of the curriculum. These are harsh words about topic work in British primary schools, but they have helped a number of people, including ourselves, to re-examine their own teaching procedures.

Concepts

Concept development, then, is not to be left to chance and in this section we propose to consider which concepts we should as teachers consciously cultivate and by what means. But before we do so we must clarify our use of language. What is meant when we say a child has or has not 'got' a concept? What happens when he forms a concept? When this is discussed in educational textbooks the authors usually take as illustrative examples the formation by young children of very simple concepts: for instance, they may show how a child, by repeatedly manipulating groups of five objects of different shapes, colours and sizes, is able to abstract the notion of 'five', apply it in a variety of new situations and learn the symbol associated with it. The concept is formed as the result of handling concrete objects. If the child has difficulty with the concept 'five' the teacher shows him 'concrete' examples of five marbles or oranges or whatever. Comparatively little is said however about the formation of concepts involving little opportunity for the child to handle materials in the classroom situation, for example concepts like family, rules, courage, growth, police and village. But many concrete experiences contribute to the formation of these concepts. For example a child has lived for years in a family, seen photographs probably of his own family, visited other families, observed animal families in pictures and at the zoo, heard stories about children in families, acted out family situations in plays and so on. He has had a number of experiences from which he has extracted the idea of family. He has been introduced to the word used for it and learned to use it in speech and writing. If you give him a number of examples and non-examples of a family, he can pick out, say, pictures showing a family and set aside those showing, say, a crowd of children in a playground. We can tell that he has a concept therefore if he can recognise an example of it; rejects a non-example; uses the concept word appropriately; and may be able to say 'This is a family: there is a mother and a father and children.' The matter of the concept word needs further consideration. It is agreed that a child (or an adult) may pick up and use a word without having a full grasp of the concept it represents: on the other hand, studies of handicapped children have shown that a child may have a concept but not know the word for it. As teachers we need to be aware of the distinction between the two states of mind. Concepts therefore are abstractions: some have concrete referents and are therefore easier for young children to grasp. The concrete referent for the concept 'family' might be the people in the child's family, a picture or photograph of them. Some concepts grasped by many children by the age of seven or eight have no concrete referent: an example of this is the concept of 'importance'. This is an abstraction used frequently in conversation, and children who can answer the question 'Which of these people in this picture is the most important?' have taken a significant step forward in intellectual development. They will, by the age of eleven or twelve, have developed a considerable number of similarly abstract ideas, but they will probably still need the prop of a practical example of the concept when they are manipulating them.

Can we say anything else about the intellectual characteristics of primary school children which is relevant to our consideration of topic work? One useful idea is that children in the concrete operational stage can probably handle four variables simultaneously. We give various examples of this later in the book. A simple one is a task which requires children to choose the best place for a vegetable garden taking into account four factors, the slope of land, the direction it faces, the position of trees casting shadows and the distance from a house. The ability to handle four variables at once is seen to be a very valuable one, and marks substantial intellectual progress.

Do we need to consider 'formal operations' which Piaget argues develop, if social conditions are appropriate, in early adolescence? By formal operations we mean the ability to handle abstractions without concrete referents, to consider and evaluate a multiplicity of possible solutions to a problem, to form and test a hypothesis. Intellectual development is not however an even process: Piaget's field was mathematics and science and people working in the field of history for example have found that, in handling historical situations remote from their experience, learners did not become capable of formal operational thinking until much later. This may however be due to a variety of factors: social and economic concepts have not been deliberately cultivated in instruction — although mathematical concepts are the central concern of maths teachers throughout the primary school. With an education focused on conceptual development perhaps more of our pupils would reach formal operations before they left school. In any case it seems likely that there will be some able children in the primary school who are on the edge of formal operational thought and may be encouraged to pass that barrier from time to time. It is as well to remember that none of us operate at the limits of our intellectual ability all the time as Piaget admitted when he described himself as reverting to pre-operational thought when he kicked the car to make it go. We need as teachers to look for the moment when the children we teach operate at the limits of their understanding as, for example, one eight year old who asked at the end of a sequence of work about the Greek gods and the myths associated with them: 'If the Greeks thought their gods existed and they didn't, could it be that we think God exists and he doesn't?' Discussing this comment with friends we found it difficult to decide whether or not this implied formal operational thought. On the one hand the child might have a very 'concrete' image of God as an old man with a white beard and, on the other, he was postulating a hypothetical situation and apparently arguing logically 'If x then y' both sophisticated forms of thought. What is important to the teacher however is not the somewhat academic problem of classifying thought as pre-operational, concrete or formal, but what response he ought to make to the child which will promote his intellectual progress. It is to this issue we propose to address ourselves in this book and, while recognising the value of Piaget's contribution to our understanding of children's thinking, we prefer not to use terminology which is in itself fraught with difficulties of definition.

Which Concepts to Select

Given that we accept the importance of concept development in children's growth, we then face the question, 'Which concepts do we cultivate and on what principles do we select them?' The most influential contributor to the argument about this has been Jerome Bruner who, in the early sixties, argued that instruction should be focused on developing 'key' concepts. He used the key metaphor advisedly, since he saw such concepts as opening doors to the understanding of the major disciplines and facilitating further learning – once a child had some grasp of a 'key' concept, other newly learned material could be related to it. Both Bruner and a number of British philosophers became interested in the 'structures' of disciplines. Once again we are using imagery: a discipline like history or geography is a highly abstract concept and does not in a literal sense have a structure in the sense that a building is said to do so. But given the metaphors, each subject is assumed to have certain characteristic concepts, keys to the further understanding of the discipline. For example key concepts in history might be continuity and change, in sociology, culture and values. Bruner himself did not claim to define these 'key' concepts, but his idea proved so exciting that in nearly every area specialists have attempted to produce their own list of these key concepts.

Since Bruner, and others too have identified in the disciplines not only key concepts but characteristic methods of inquiry which could also be learned and applied to new situations, it might be expected that this movement would stimulate the teaching of the traditional school subjects and discourage interdisciplinary work. Some disciplines however are found to use certain concepts in common: for example the concept of culture is not unique to sociology and consequently 'topic' type work can flourish under this new philosophy. Having identified supposedly the 'key' concepts of the discipline, inevitably educationists began to attempt to translate the ideas into work for children. What 'key' concepts should children learn in primary school and how could curricula be constructed round them? A number of interesting attempts have been made to do this by Bruner himself in *Man, a course of study*, by Hilda Taba in California and subsequently in England in the Schools Council projects such as *Place, Time and Society* and *Social Studies 8-13, Schools Council Working Paper 39*.

Inseparable from the idea of key concepts is that of the spiral curriculum. By this Bruner means that children will first encounter key ideas and concepts in a primitive form in early childhood, and will re-encounter them in more highly developed forms in their subsequent work in schools, each encounter leading to a more sophisticated understanding. For example, K.D. Wann shows how pre-school children may encounter the idea of 'development' by collecting pictures of old cars and sequencing them. This embryonic understanding might be strengthened in the primary school by topic work on transport or houses and, in the secondary school, first by work on the Industrial Revolution and still later by a study of revolutions. So the concept is basically the same but it is applied to different and increasingly complex materials. Examples of the detailed development of a spiral curriculum are to be found in the work of Hilda Taba who devised interesting social studies curricula in Californian schools for children aged 6-12. The difficulty with 'spirals' that straddle several years of a child's school life is that they appear to involve centrally controlled or collectively agreed curricula, which have not yet recommended themselves to the British tradition. We therefore think it more helpful to suggest that teachers might find out what level of understanding of a concept children have and attempt to take them one step further up the rungs of understanding. For example, if we take the concept 'family' as an example of a key sociological idea, 'the human group', on entering school a child may understand that a family consists of mother, father and children but not that a family is an economic unit i.e. that the adult members work to provide not just Saturday treats but shelter, food and clothing for the group. The teacher can therefore take the child that step up the spiral, but may not yet introduce notions like nuclear and extended families or clans and tribes which are largely groups of related families.

As previously mentioned, Bruner claims that his approach to teaching the concepts and skills which characterise a discipline means that the foundations of any subject can be taught to anybody at any age in an intellectually respectable form. If this is so, there is no need to limit 'topic' work in primary schools to the subjects traditional in our schools such as history and geography, and children will be capable of learning the elements of sociology, politics, economics and psychology. If this sounds outrageous it may be more palatable to say that children can learn about the groups to which they belong: for example, families – as outlined in Hilda Taba's *Social Studies Curriculum* for six year olds, their peer groups – street communities as in *Social Studies 8-13*, they can discuss the nature of authority if it is approached, say, through work on Uniforms; work on Shops need not be solely a mathematical exercise but can involve an understanding of trade, and psychology can be approached by way of a study of how animals and people learn. We accept wholeheartedly the idea that we have tended to underestimate what children can learn if, as Bruner says, we are courteous enough to translate it into terms they can understand.

There remains however the very difficult matter of choice of what concepts can be cultivated in the limited time available for work in schools. Even the supposed key concepts of the disciplines are numerous and, once the detailed planning of units of work begins, more and more concepts may be thrown up. And what about the concepts which cannot easily be attached to any single discipline, e.g. importance, function, majority, minority, ambiguity, etc? Bruner argues that what is taught should be worth an adult's knowing. But the question of what is 'worthwhile' requires a value judgement on the part of the teacher. It is an individual decision. We ourselves have made such judgements in the course of this book: we cannot however determine what other people's choices should be. We do however argue that it is the teacher who makes the selection of concepts to be cultivated, that it requires serious thought and discussion well ahead and, as will be demonstrated, we would not wish to leave their cultivation to chance.

Here we should admit that we firmly believe that the teacher plans and directs the process of instruction. To some teachers this may appear to be a retrograde step. Teachers who have been influenced by the 'progressive' movement in education may feel that they should start from the interests demonstrated by the children and follow their initiatives. We think there are weaknesses in this position. 'Topic' work supposedly arising from the interests of children tends to be surprisingly stereotyped because, we might suggest, teachers find in children the interests they hope and expect to find. No child admits to an interest in smashing up telephone booths, and if a child voiced an interest in sexual behaviour, how many teachers would be prepared to follow it up in topic work? Teachers too, looking for initiatives among their children, may seize on the interest of one child but be unable to find any expressed interest in particularly apathetic and unresponsive children who are not prepared to initiate activity. In the case of such children the teacher's role is to provide experiences which will extend limited horizons and provoke questions. Once he or she does this there is little difference between the progressive's philosophical position and our own. A series of topics supposedly based on children's interests may well be unbalanced, omitting some vital subject area like science, or repetitive, neither of which flaws would be tolerable in such areas of the curriculum as mathematics or language. Other teachers have based topic work entirely on their own enthusiasms since here they have a command of the material and the possibility of communicating their own commitment: this is open to very similar criticisms. A whole year's work on say, canals does not seem to us to be justified and when it is argued that through canals, maths, science, history and geography will be 'brought in', these disciplines are apt to appear in the form of bits of relevant information without necessarily involving the development of their conceptual structures or relevant skills.

Strategies for Encouraging Concept Development

If we are teaching to secure conceptual growth we need to show how this may be done. Here we can suggest a variety of strategies, some of which apply only to certain kinds of concept. One approach is that suggested by Marion Blank who devised it for pre-school children — but it can be applied nearly as well with older children. She suggests that as an early step we should list the attributes of a concept. We have already encountered this in discussing family: one attribute of the family is that it consists of people related by marriage and blood; another that a family may make common decisions; another than it is an economic unit. In listing attributes we are in effect analysing the concept, an exacting task which is also discussed under evaluation (see Chapter 3). A harder example might be culture: here a sociological dictionary helps us to decide that a number of things make up the characteristics of a culture — tools; values; beliefs; economy; etc. Immediately we come up against the problem that we are using language unfamiliar to children and even difficult for some adults. We need therefore to find what Blank calls 'verbal mediators' for the concepts. Instead of using, culture, values, economy, we say 'way of life', 'what they think important', 'how they earn their living'.

Exercise 1

Perhaps you could try to devise verbal mediators for authority, power,
unemployment, inflation, factory, justice and revenge. Finding verbal
mediators sounds imposingly difficult but it is in fact what the good
teacher does all the time and once practised it soon becomes instinctive.

A next step is to present an example of the concept using the verbal
mediator, if the concept word is unfamiliar. With young children this
might mean presenting a picture saying 'Here is a family' or 'Here are
men working in a factory'. A visit too might 'present the example' of
the concept. If the concept is more difficult, say 'way of life', it may
take a whole unit of work on one example of a people's way of life,
e.g. on Eskimos, to present the example which would be built up
gradually by pictures, stories and reading materials. Then having looked
at houses, clothes, travel and ways of obtaining food, the teacher might
ask the children to make a frieze and then attach to it the caption 'This
is the Eskimo's way of life'. With some kinds of concept the teacher
may present both examples of the concept and non-examples: 'This is
not a factory but a shop', 'This is not a factory but a home'.

The presentation of the concept can be discussed so as to bring out
some of its attributes. For example having shown the picture of the
factory, one might say: 'What are they doing?', 'Why do you think they
are doing it?', 'Does your father do this kind of work?' A young child
cannot be expected to form a concept solely from one example (though
experienced adolescent learners are often expected, perhaps unreason-
ably, to do this). Consequently it is necessary to provide several
examples of the concept, possibly by drawing on the children's own
experience – 'You belong to a family. How many are there in your
family?' or 'Let us make a picture of our way of life. Draw me a picture to show your house, clothes and food etc., and label it "My way
of life".' Alternatively by providing a contrasting example, e.g. a
picture of an animal family and a study of American Indians, we seek
the same goal.

Some authors would suggest that when the children have had several
examples of a concept they should be encouraged by questioning to
infer the characteristics of the concept, rejecting fortuitous or irrelevant
matter in the examples so that the children might say, for instance,
after work on families that a family usually has father, mother and
children. Others argue that the teacher should himself give this kind of
comment when presenting the example. 'By way of life we mean the
homes people live in, the clothes they wear, the work they do.' When

children appear to have a grasp of the concept they may be given practice in recognising positive and rejecting negative examples of it. For example, if children have encountered the concept of 'habitat', they might be asked to sort out pictures showing the habitats of different creatures and separating them from those pictures which were irrelevant. A final word on negative examples of concepts; children find it more difficult to reject negative examples than select positive examples. If we show a picture of a dog scampering about the sands and ask 'Is the dog working?' the children may be unwilling to say 'No' because the form of question suggests the answer 'Yes'. The ability to reject irrelevant material in any context is however a valuable one and needs teaching. Children need to learn that a negative response can be the right response and will only do so if they have practice, reinforced by the teacher's approval.

When children recognise positive and reject negative examples of concepts they may need to be introduced to the concept word if it has not already been used conversationally. Sometimes teachers spend quite a lot of time studying a group of people – the Greeks, Bushmen or whatever and the children learn a lot about their culture, but the teacher lets it go at that. If he does so he fails to extract the maximum amount from the experience for he has laboured to build up a concept without giving its name and getting the children to use it. He would be well advised to say 'Well now, we have learned about the Greeks: we have made a picture showing them worshipping their gods, playing their games, sailing their ships. All this we call their way of life . . .' And having introduced this useful verbal mediator, he needs to get the children to use it in tasks and discussion. 'What is good about their way of life? Would you like it? How is it different from ours?' Some people would in fact argue that the best way to promote concept development is to provide the experiences from which the concept can be inferred and only provide the new concept word as the coping stone of the edifice.

Since a concept is in fact a way of classifying a group of phenomena ('loyalty' for example is a concept-word which classifies certain kinds of behaviour) it follows that classification exercises are helpful. If we ask children to list what they will need to stay alive on a desert island we are teaching the concept 'survival'. If we ask children to list all that is needed to build, stock and run a supermarket (as Hilda Taba did) they can then be asked to group those things which go together. When they put together hammer, spade, shovel, they may be able to suggest a common name – all these are tools. When they say they will need vans and lorries, they may or may not be able to classify these as transport. When they say they will need people at the check out, people to fill shelves, someone to tell people what to do, they are unlikely to call these people 'labour' but may use a verbal mediator and say 'people to do the work'. Such listing, grouping and naming activities are all helpful for concept development. An alternative form of classification exercise for older children who have some grasp of a concept and need to refine it may involve giving them examples and non-examples in written form. 'John and James go to France for a holiday. Are they making a colony? People from Ireland come to work in England. Are they making a colony? The answers here may well refine the children's understanding of colony: it is permanent, not temporary, it involves a group of people who live close together, not scattered about the country.

This second method also utilises mismatch situations, which involves valuable techniques for raising the level of children's under-standing, and enables the teacher to identify the level of understanding the child has. If in answer to a question about a factory a child says, drawing on his knowledge of the only factory he knows, 'It's that place down the road where they make bicycles', the teacher needs to provide an example of a factory which makes, say, biscuits, so that the child assimilates this new experience and is able to raise his level of under-standing of 'factory', saying that it is a place where things are made. The teacher cannot of course organise a visit to a factory on an occasion like this so he may ask other children for their understanding of factory and in discussion encourage them all to accommodate the newly shared experience. A good deal of a teacher's informal conversations with children as he goes about a class involves the use of mismatch situations. Consider this small example of teacher-child conversation.

(Invasion)
Teacher: What is an invasion?
Pupil: It is a kind of attack.
Teacher: If you attacked Jim would that be an invasion?
Pupil: No. Lots of people have to come to your country.
Teacher: If they come for a holiday is that an invasion?
Pupil: No, not unless you didn't want them to come.
Teacher: So an invasion is . . .

In the following discussion the teacher has been talking to the 6-year-old children about work, and has established that people work to make

money to feed their families. She then introduces a mismatch situation
by showing first a picture of Morris dancers and then one of footballers.

Teacher: Do you think they are working?

Jess, Noel, Calvin, Cathy: Yes.

Others.   No.

Cathy: They are dancing and people give money to them.

Teacher: I see, if you get money they are working . . .?

Jess, Noel: No.

Others: Yes.

Teacher: So you don't work at school, because you don't get paid?

Jess: No we do work at school but we don't get any money
because we are too young. It is work to learn not work to
earn.

Marion: Not all work is paid.

(Here the new idea is assimilated by Marion)

Teacher shows a picture of footballers.

Teacher: Do these men earn money?

Calvin: They're playing football and they win things and get money.

Teacher: What happens in summer when they don't play football?

Mark: They still get paid because they have to practice . . .

Noel: Some people play sport for fun and some get paid. It is a
sort of work when they get paid.

(Noel assimilates the new idea)

These conversations involve the repeated use of mismatch technique so
as to develop conceptual grasp.

We have perhaps given enough examples to show that in promoting
conceptual development in young children, you begin with the 'concrete' and move nearer to the abstract. By concrete we do not mean as
we should in maths that the children should manipulate real objects
and necessarily therefore encourage them to spend lots of time cutting
out cardboard for castle or swords when teaching 'way of life' for
instance. Moving near to the concrete may however mean referring to
things children have touched, used, experienced or observed, for example
breaking down 'way of life' to mean initially homes, clothes, food and
work. In particular it may mean getting nearer to children's day-to-day
experience; for example authority may be personified in policemen or
lollipop ladies; laws in yellow lines forbidding parking; rules in those
children have learned about crossing roads; the community in the
streets in which they live; trade in the swapping of children's collected

objects; revenge in their own feelings about 'getting their own back'; agriculture in a visit to a farm. It requires some ingenuity to make some concepts accessible to children. If we take the concept 'values', we have a difficult idea which one might consider impossible to approach until the late secondary stage. It is not however impossible if we make it 'concrete' by saying: 'How did the Eskimos treat old people? What did the Greeks spend their money on? What did they prefer to do with their spare time? Which did the Elizabethans build most, churches or houses? And how are these various forms of behaviour different from ours? What does it suggest about us if we give elderly people pensions or if we spend our money on holidays and travel, etc.?'

Some difficult notions can be incorporated in stories which make the abstract concrete. Here is an example:

Exercise 2

What concepts are being cultivated here?
Tom kitten is six weeks old. When he was born he began to feed from his mother straight away, nobody needed to teach him what to do. Soon he began to stagger about the box he was born in. Now that he is seven weeks old his mistress says its time he learned to lap. She puts out a saucer of just warm milk. Taking him to the milk she pushes his nose into it. He splutters. He has milk all over his whiskers and starts to wash his face. He tastes the milk. Not bad at all. In a day or two he has learned to lap like a grown-up cat.

It is much harder to learn to get through the cat-door. His mistress decides to teach him. First she opens it wide. He can jump in and out. A few days later, she opens it quite a lot but he has to wriggle through. To encourage him she rattles his plate and when he has wriggled through she gives him a reward, a bit of chicken. Soon he can get in and out of the house through his own door. He learns to wriggle through without trapping his tail.

So some things any kitten knows how to do; others someone has to teach him.

Not only can a concept be presented to the children in the form of a picture but in making a frieze or collage or composite picture a concept can be built up and made 'concrete'. Such a picture might show 'way of life', 'community' or 'environment' as we show later in the book.

Finally, we would argue that while secondary teachers tend to overestimate the capacity of their pupils to handle abstract ideas, primary school teachers tend to underestimate what their pupils know and understand and what they are capable of doing. We have ourselves been frequently surprised by the way children, at reaching school age, have absorbed a knowledge of their environment. American investigators were similarly surprised by the wide number of countries and places their 6-year-old subjects had visited and by the wealth of knowledge they had assimilated from television, so that for instance they already associated India with poverty, starvation and overpopulation. The investigators found the children capable of dealing with sequential if not chronological time and of developing social science concepts. We ourselves have found that a majority of the 6-year-olds in a class on a council estate school had visited a bank and knew that you got money there. A minority knew that in order to get money out you had to put it in. Seven year olds were able to say, after looking at a picture of an African woman with her baby, 'It is a poor country' — in other words, they could grasp at not only the notion of a poor person but a poor society. Children in that age group knew all about what happened when you were out of work and how you got the money to live. Some even younger children volunteered in another context that their parents paid money to pay for the school. One could multiply such examples but perhaps the best thing we can do is to suggest that you find out for yourself exactly what the children you teach know and understand. There is advice on how to do this in Part Three.

Notes on Exercises

Exercise 1

Possible verbal mediators for concepts

Authority	Who is in charge? Who tells people what to do?
Power	Who is the leader? Who is the boss?
	Who makes people do things?
Unemployment	Cannot find work.
	Has no work to do.
Inflation	Prices go up.
Factory	A place people go to make things.
Justice	Is it fair?
Revenge	Getting your own back.

Exercise 2

The story of the kitten and the cat-door is teaching the ideas of innate behaviour (feeding, moving, washing) and learned behaviour (lapping, getting through the cat-door). One could follow up such a story with a listing exercise: list those things a cat/puppy does without being taught and then make a list of those things he can learn to do. After the listing exercise the teacher could introduce the words 'innate' and 'learned' as applied to behaviour.

2 SKILLS

When Bruner and others analyse the nature of knowledge they identify as important not only concepts but characteristic modes of inquiry. Just as we noted the concepts characteristic of each discipline we can outline the methods used by historians, geographers, sociologists, economists and psychologists. For example, in politics the student of elections may start with a question he wishes to investigate: who is likely to win the next election? He questions a carefully constructed sample of people and from their answers makes a forecast suggesting what is likely to happen. The modes of inquiry of a number of disciplines involve the same steps, the selection of an area of investigation or a problem; the construction of a questionnaire, the selection of a sample, the analysis of the resulting data using mathematical techniques, and the publication of a conclusion. In some areas, for example in psychology, the heart of the investigation may be an experiment. Bruner argues that if children are inducted into such techniques they not only learn a set of skills transferable to the solution of other similar problems, but they learn to make tentative conclusions and do not mistake interpretations for facts.

Already in many schools when children carry out a traffic survey or similar small scale survey they are being inducted into a mode of inquiry of this kind. Later in the book we suggest that children might investigate attitudes to work by way of a questionnaire. If they do so, they are likely to come to conclusions such as 'Most people prefer to work'. They will know exactly how soundly that conclusion is based from the investigation they carried out, they will know perhaps that it is based on a small sample, that they were not able to ask people from every occupation, and that a minority of people did not prefer to work. They will learn therefore the limitations of the statement they make and will express it tentatively as Bruner anticipated. They will also have acquired useful skills — making a questionnaire; perhaps recording the results on a graph, and publishing, if only to the school at large, a series of conclusions couched with a respect for truth.

The idea of teaching the mode of inquiry has influenced a number of secondary school curricular innovations and, as we have seen, has had an influence on primary school work. Some history teachers in primary schools have attempted to introduce children to the historians' way of working by carrying out small investigations in local history using a variety of evidence including documents. While we agree that it is valuable for the children to be introduced to the idea of evidence and to evaluate certain kinds of evidence, we do not propose to explore this kind of innovation fully partly because excellent examples are already available in, for example, *Teaching History* and partly because the use of historical evidence is very difficult for the non-specialist teachers who have never been taught in this way themselves and we are addressing ourselves essentially to non-specialist general practitioners. But a further consideration is that we would not wish to make teaching the mode of inquiry in any discipline our major objective in primary school topic work. In history particularly it could lead to such aberrations – as we see them – as teaching children palaeography so that they may read documents written in the handwriting of earlier centuries. Further we would argue that the best basis for subsequent work in any discipline in the secondary school is to develop in children the *conceptual* tools they need for understanding the subject and a wide range of all purpose intellectual skills.

The idea of such all-purpose thinking skills was first popularised by Bloom *et al.*, in *Taxonomy of Educational Objectives*. Like many others, we have found this powerfully influential and have gone on to modify Bloom to produce our own way of categorising intellectual skills and the questions, tasks and various activities which encourage their development. We would not however claim that the categories we use: interpretation, classification, extrapolation, evaluation, etc., which are discussed in the next chapter, are the only possible ones or that it is a matter of great moment exactly how a particular question or response is classified. And we part company from Bloom *et al.* when they order the skills into a hierarchy with the simple (e.g. translation) near the lower end and the more difficult (e.g. evaluation) near the top of the scale. We have found that tasks involving all the skills may be set at varying levels of difficulty. If one says to a pre-school child 'What will happen if you get this clean tee-shirt dirty?' he will be able to 'guess' the outcome and say 'Mummy may be cross'. If we ask an older child to extrapolate about the effects of pollution on the environment we are setting a more exacting task, because the concepts involved are so much harder, not because the skill involved is different.

Some people may think that young children are not capable of practising intellectual skills. The work of Blank and Solomon however shows that even disadvantaged pre-school children could, with appropriate questioning, be taught to make inferences. For example, the children were ultimately able to interpret the teacher's action in putting on her coat and conjecture that she was going home. British children have usually learned to interpret pictures and photographs well before they come to school and can answer questions like 'What is happening in the picture?' Children and even adults from certain primitive societies could not do this.

Consider this conversation between a mother and her 3-year-old son:

Mother: Which dinosaurs do you know?
Paul: I know Brontosaurus.
Mother: Hmmm. What else?
Paul: Strykosaurus. (Strachosaurus)
Mother: Yes. What else?
Paul: Stegosaurus. And Brontosaurus.
Mother: Yes, you said that.
Paul: Tyrannosaurus Rex. And Stryko – and Triceratops.
Mother: That's right. Which is your favourite? (evaluative question)
Paul: I think – uh – Tyrannosaurus Rex.
Mother: Why is he your favourite? Why is he your favourite?
            (asks for reasons for evaluation)
Paul: He wins everybody!
Mother: He wins! Who does he win?
Paul: He wins Triceratops, but he still dies. (referring to episode
            in the book)
Mother: Does he! Ummm.
Paul: Then Allocaurus wins but he dies. Then nobody wins.
Mother: What happened to the dinosaurs? Can you tell me? What
            happened to the dinosaurs?
Paul: Maybe they all had a fight with – uh – maybe the plant
            eaters had a fight, and the meat eaters had a fight with each
            other. That's what they did, or the earth growed too cold.
Mother: Yes, maybe the earth grew too cold. Do you think so?
Paul: No one knows.
Mother: No, no one knows, do they. No one knows.
Paul: Maybe the dinosaurs know – how they died.
Mother: It's difficult to ask them though, isn't it . . . if they're dead.
            What happens to dinosaurs when they die, do you think?
Paul: Um . . . dinosaurs die.
Mother: Yes, and what happens to them? Do you know?
Paul: No, they just get buried.
Mother: Yes, and then what happens?
Paul: And they get took away in a funeral car.[1]

Although this little boy is still prone to magical interpretations of his world he can answer an evaluation question, 'Which is your favourite?' and give a reason for his choice. He is also learning to demonstrate the tentativeness Bruner valued, is able to envisage several possibilities and accept uncertainty.

Children then can demonstrate that they possess these skills in embryonic form. Why practise them in school? First of all teachers are aware that simply teaching information in topic work is not enough. How many of us can recall the details of what we learned in history and geography in the primary school and if we could, in what sense would it be useful to us? Teachers wish to give their pupils something of permanent value and, in their search for this, they have sometimes laid great emphasis on the acquisition of reference skills, the ability to use books to find out what we wish to know, to handle encyclopedias and/or dictionaries, tables of contents and indices. These skills are valuable but not a totally satisfying answer to the teacher's problem. While these skills are useful to a student in, say secondary school and undergraduate studies, not all the problems of adult life can be solved by consulting a book though that may be a useful first step. Teachers universally wish to teach their pupils to think – and to know from their own experience that the ability to do so is the most useful byproduct of school life. They are often however at a loss about how to help children to perform this mysterious process and exhortations to 'Think, John, think' do not have the hoped for outcome. The idea of a series of thinking strategies, each of which can be initiated by different kinds of question or task, can therefore be perceived as a valuable step forward.

There are two other reasons why we would recommend practice in intellectual skills. First, having acquired a concept a child needs to use it, skills and concepts are then essentially linked, not disparate. Skills can hardly be practised in a vacuum: you cannot practise interpretation for example without interpreting something. Concepts too need to be used if they are to be accommodated into the child's permanent intellectual structure. Learning skills and concepts are therefore complementary activities and should go hand in hand. For example, if the child has been introduced to work on Authority in the context say of matters within his own experience: the school, the neighbourhood, the peer group and has been introduced to the concept word 'authority' one might say to him, 'Which of these people is in authority here?', 'Which have authority to stop the traffic?', 'Which sort of things does a doctor have authority to do'. All these are exercises in classification. We might go on to ask him to extrapolate: 'If you had the authority to run the school, what changes would you make?', 'Which of the children in this story is best fitted to hold authority?' (evaluation).

Finally there is evidence to show that children's ability to handle tasks involving intellectual skills can be improved with experience. This has been shown by a variety of educational experiments ranging from that of Black and Solomon with young children to eleven-year-old children's ability to make moral judgements by Kohlberg. It is however virtually self-evident; if one introduces children to say questions involving the interpretation of a picture, they may be a little thrown by an unfamiliar approach but they usually show rapid even dramatic improvement which, as you would expect, subsequently becomes slower and more difficult to detect over the fairly long term.

Questioning

Since intellectual skills may be brought into play by appropriate questions, it seems desirable to comment on the technique of asking them. A study of teaching in the lower forms of secondary schools has shown that teachers tend to use predominantly closed questions involving factual recall. An example of such questions would be 'How many legs has the spider?' or 'What was the date of the Norman Conquest?' Such questions induce responses which are right or wrong and tell the teacher something he knows very well already. Open-ended questions however like the ones shown in the previous discussion and in the conversation about work on page 26, e.g. 'Do people enjoy their jobs?', do not usually produce answers that invite ticks or crosses, require elaborated responses rather than monosyllabic ones, and invite tentativeness. The six-year-old children's responses to 'Do people enjoy their jobs?' were 'Sometimes', 'Daddy often says he's tired' and 'People have to work so they can get money but they don't like it all the time'. The answers to the open-ended questions are often varied, genuinely interesting to the teacher, and provide material which the teacher can develop so as to secure progress. They also demonstrate the tentativeness Bruner valued. It is sometimes assumed that children are made unhappy by uncertainty or to feel more secure with things in black and white — even though the teacher knows them to be grey. *Social Studies 8-13* talks about getting children 'to tolerate ambiguity'. It may be that they do not have trouble with tentativeness unless their school experience leads them to feel that to say 'I don't know' or 'I'm not sure' is a manifestation of failure rather than a recognition of the limitations of human knowledge.

One way for a teacher to improve his oral questioning is to use a tape recorder and analyse his interaction with his pupils, studying not only his contributions but their responses. Interaction analysis has however been discussed at great length elsewhere so that we do not propose to explore it further. It will be clear however that these techniques have influenced our approach to teaching, in particular our approach to discussion, the importance of which in the mental development of young children is now well appreciated and which we consider at length from page 102.

Transfer

Implicit in a good deal of what we say is the idea of transfer, i.e. that the understanding of concepts and skills acquired at one stage of education can be transferred by the learner to new situations encountered at a later date. The notion of transfer is at the heart of Bruner's thesis that we should teach the structures of subjects not information. Much information is highly specific to one situation, e.g. the names of dinosaurs once learned are not likely to be used again unless a teacher asks for dinosaurs' names.But generalisations such as 'When people emigrate their way of life is likely to change' or 'When the supply of goods increases the price of them is likely to fall' can be transferred from the situation in which they were learned to new situations both inside and outside the classroom. A concept like 'evolution' once learned can enable a learner to interpret and organise a wide variety of data not only in the field of biology but in other disciplines too. Some people distrust the idea of the transfer of learning from one situation to another because, many years ago, it was agreed that the learning by rote of nonsense syllables did not improve the memory, but if we did not constantly transfer our learning from one situation to another, we should be likely to burn our hands or get knocked down crossing roads. It is thought however that learning is transferred only if the situation in which it took place and the situation where it is to be applied subsequently are similar. Transfer is also facilitated if teachers teach for it, i.e. if they encourage the learner to reflect upon how, say, he solved a problem, so that the principles involved are made explicit. This seems to be the technique used by de Bono in his curricular materials designed to teach thinking.

If we try to provide an example from our own domain: suppose in the context of a topic on building the children have considered the influence of three factors on the homes of Red Indians viz materials, climate and way of life, the teacher could well conclude by reminding them of these three considerations and say 'Next time you are thinking about homes, remember to ask yourself "What was there for them to use to build with?", "What kinds of weather did the house have to stand up to?" and "How did the people in the houses live?" ' Consequently when the children come to examine the homes of some other group, say Iron Age people in Britain, the teacher will remind them of these key questions and concepts. It might therefore be helpful for us, instead of starting a lesson with a banal reminder of past learning: 'What did we learn last time about X?', to make a habit of reminding children of useful and relevant concepts and techniques, e.g.: 'You remember when we made a list of what we needed for the supermarket, we first listed, then grouped and then labelled the groups, now today we are going to make a list of what we need to survive on a desert island . . .' or alternatively: 'You remember when we listed the pros and cons of living in a cave, now we are going to think about the pros and cons of living in a lake village.'

Note

1. We are indebted to our colleague Dr Sandra Harris for permission to use this transcript.

3 ATTITUDES AND MORAL DEVELOPMENT

Learners' Attitudes

Attitude formation in children is a potentially explosive subject. A number of young teachers when asked what attitudes they would wish to cultivate in children said unhesitatingly 'respect for authority'. When asked to list the kinds of behaviour which children would show if they did respect authority, they naturally referred to the children's behaviour in the classroom. It was only when they went on to ask such questions as 'Are they to obey all orders given by an authority?', 'Are they to believe everything they are told by an authority?', 'Are they to believe everything they read in a printed authority?' that they perceived that they, as responsible members of a democratic society, wished to cultivate a very complex set of attitudes which they had not thought through fully. And it soon became clear that attitudes to authority were concerned not only with feelings but with under-standing. In other words feeling and thinking were closely linked.

There are, however, certain attitudes relevant to children's work which are less controversial and less linked to levels of understanding. Some essential attitudes we take for granted in the majority of children, i.e. willingness to attend school and, at a higher level, willingness to participate in the activities provided there. In the context of topic work we can define our goals for learners in the 'affective domain' — as this area of feelings and attitudes is known. We would wish them to be willing to ask questions relevant to the matter in hand, to make contributions to discussion, to show enthusiasm by, for example, choosing to read relevant books in their spare time. Behaviour of this kind demonstrates a developing interest in the work which may, as the child matures, become incorporated into his personality permanently, though we should accept that he may form many such interests which prove transient though not necessarily without value for him. Reflection suggests that the growth of such interests, which we have all experi-enced, is fostered by success and the satisfactions involved in a given activity. The areas of the curriculum associated with pain and failure tend not surprisingly to be those learners avoid. Teachers therefore can encourage the growth of commitment by the generous use of praise and appreciation of children's efforts in topic work and by so carefully structuring tasks that children encounter success. This means setting the right level of difficulty in work (see Part 3), and also means that when children do encounter failure or difficulty it is dealt with constructively: that the teacher can diagnose the child's problem and do something about it (discussed in Part 3). The child's willingness to persist in the face of difficulty can be strengthened, not only by verbal encouragement from the teacher, but also if he can be rewarded by finding that his persistence does produce satisfaction, however delayed.

Many schools in the past 20 years have stressed the importance of cultivating attitudes of co-operation among children. Sometimes the chief token of this is the arrangement of desks in groups rather than rows, a feature which may characterise even classrooms where all the tasks set are in fact individual, involving little or no 'co-operation'. Children are very quick to learn from the 'hidden' curriculum and where the lesson which that 'curriculum' teaches is that people ought to compete, not co-operate, they are quick to put their arms protectively round their work or carry out disapproved forms of co-operation like copying. When they demonstrate these behaviours their attitudes, whatever their teachers' avowed goals, have been shaped by the competitive atmosphere of the school and society. If teachers wish children to show willingness to co-operate with other children, it is not enough to give different groups different work-cards, tasks or materials. What is needed is to identify certain tasks as co-operative, consider what sort of co-operation is required and teach such co-operative strategies. In devising these it may be helpful to observe what happens when a group of children spontaneously co-operate in a task or game.

Suppose the co-operative task is that of making a model of the street the children have been studying. Co-operation will be promoted if the children embarking on this are friends and choose to work together. Any form of group work can be damaged by personality clashes between individuals or if the children are effectively strangers to each other.

The task can be broken down into sub-tasks; drawing the plan on the base; listing the buildings, traffic, people observed in the street; deciding which to include; deciding, however tentatively, the proportions of the buildings to people; selecting the relevant materials; making the individual items; arranging the whole on the base; and labelling the model. All this gives scope for some group and some individual tasks. The children can co-operate in a variety of ways for example by carrying out a joint listing exercise. The teacher can help by suggesting the children sit in a group facing each other, that one volunteer writes down the items, that all children in turn make a suggestion, and that

the scribe reads it aloud for them to check it at the end. When it comes
to the decision about the items to be included and those to be omitted,
the teacher may suggest each child makes a suggestion and gives a
reason, e.g. 'The factory is the biggest building so it must be in'. It may
be desirable to advise a group of children who fall into dispute about a
decision to vote and introduce to them the notion of majority and
minority. When they reach the point of arranging the items on the
plan, they can be given an example of generous appreciation of their
efforts by the teacher. 'Hasn't Jane made a splendid factory? You can
see the people working.' The teacher can similarly set the example of
rewarding helpful suggestions from members of the group and inviting
the children to appreciate the efforts of others. There is no guarantee
that these procedures will counteract successfully all the pressures
inside and outside school towards competitive rather than co-operative
attitudes. What these suggestions illustrate is that the need for careful,
structured, thoughtful planning exists in the 'attitude' field as in any
other.

We have considered the development of favourable attitudes to
topic work and the attitudes towards learning which teachers consider
desirable, there are however attitudes to the nature of knowledge which
innovators in the field of the curriculum have come to stress recently.
We have already referred to 'tentativeness' which is valued by Bruner
and others influenced by him. But how, you might say, can we tell when
a child is demonstrating this attitude? It can often be identified when
children use words like 'probably', 'perhaps', 'it might be that' or 'do
you think that . . .' and avoid unjustified certainties. To this we would
add the willingness to say, where appropriate 'We don't know whether
. . .' – in other words to accept that there are limitations to human
knowledge. We would hope to encourage children to be willing to give
reasons for an opinion, to be willing to admit error, to be willing to
change their minds if convinced by evidence or argument, but to be
sufficiently independent not to change their opinion simply because
their best friend has a different one, in other words we would wish to
cultivate progress towards rational autonomy.

A tall order, you may say, for primary school children. How is it to
be done? First of all by example. The teacher in these circumstances
is not unwilling to say 'I don't know. Let's try to find out . . .' in
answer to a question. But going beyond that he may say, 'I don't
know. I don't think anyone knows . . .' or he may indicate several
possible explanations for a problem. He will from time to time use the
formula, 'Well, on the one hand it might be that . . . on the other hand it

might be . . . What do you think?' And he can encourage the desired attitudes by praise, by showing interest in children's tentative suggestions, by asking for alternative views, explanations and possibilities. In fact he can set tasks which evoke the attitudes desired. In the following chapters there are many illustrations of such exercises,for example nearly all open-ended questions may invite tentativeness, especially questions involving extrapolation and evaluation, e.g. 'What would happen in England if the climate suddenly became very much warmer?' or 'Which of these houses is the best?'

Some teacher may feel strongly that topic work is where the teacher can do something constructive to tackle current social problems at their roots by, for example, discouraging racist attitudes. If you have read the results of recent research which shows that children develop racist and class attitudes as young as four years old, you may feel a moral obligation to try to promote a belief in the intrinsic value of all indiviuals regardless of skin colour or sex or class. Indeed any primary school teacher cannot help but wonder if he has a duty to seek to influence children's attitudes in this field either through direct exhortation or less directly through topic work. There is evidence to suggest however that direct attempts by liberal-minded teachers to change attitudes to race may in fact be counterproductive. They could generate tension in a racially mixed class of children and create difficulties which did not previously exist. We ourselves would prefer to approach this question obliquely rather than head on. For example work on Red Indians might provide a chance to examine racial clashes without raising the emotional temperature. In the context of a subject therefore where the *matter* is distanced, we would ask such questions as 'What would the Indians feel when the white men killed the buffalo?' 'What did the white settlers feel about the Indians?' 'Why did they fear them?'

Another topic which might lend itself to work on race might be one on 'people moving'. When children had considered what moving house meant to them (How do you feel about leaving friends? How do you feel the first day at a new school?), then one might consider different groups of emigrants: the Pilgrim Fathers; British emigrants going to Australia, West Indians coming to England; etc. The teacher might organise children to work on different migrant groups using the same set of questions: 'Why do they go? What problems do they have when they get there? How do they feel about their old homes, the new land?' etc. From such work the children might begin to appreciate the difficulties and aspirations of people entering British society.

Whether or not we teachers undertake this kind of topic it is important we should be sensitive to and critical of reading material which obliquely inculcates racist or sexist values. Readers in which coloured people appear only as primitive tribesmen are still encountered, as are histories which treat the story of the Americans, say, as a tale of white conquest and scarcely refer to the culture of the indigenous population, their cities, their art, their economies. Books on jobs and careers rarely show girls in anything but traditionally feminine roles and abound with assumptions which some people would call 'sexist'. Similarly the same principles apply in planning topics, a topic, for six year olds, on 'Work', should not necessarily begin with a discussion of 'What does Daddy do?' in a society where working mothers are a common experience and a topic on India will be more concerned with Akbar ar Ghandi than with Clive.

Not only do children form attitudes to race which they catch from those of adults, but they are known to form favourable attitudes to government, admiring the Queen for instance and being firmly on the side of law and order. It has been found that well before adolescence children are beginning to form a commitment to one party or another, before the age for instance at which one would expect to find a full understanding of what a political party is. And even more important they are forming attitudes favourable or unfavourable to participation in the democratic process and community life. This seems to us to justify our including in the children's programme topics like 'authority' or 'justice' or 'the community'. They are not, as many have supposed, outside children's range of interests if presented appropriately.

It was knowledge of American research on the growth of social and political attitudes among children which helped to make Vincent Rogers feel that British primary schools were unduly prone to censor social studies materials so as to exclude the controversial. Children, he thought, were encouraged to list the services provided by the community but not to evaluate them, to make traffic censuses but not to consider critically the problems created by the motor car. Altogether they are fed too bland an intellectual diet. This is a serious and, we think, justified criticism. We would go further and argue that commonly the approach to topics is sentimental. For instance 'people who help us' is a popular theme with seven-year-olds. The people who 'help us' such as dustmen are in fact very often comparatively poorly paid employees doing an unpleasant, heavy and dirty job in the service sector of the economy. The type of question we might ask about them is not only how do they 'help' us but what would happen if nobody did this work, is it more or less important than that of the milkman or postman or the farmer, and what are the advantages and disadvantages of the job from the point of view of those who do it? This same sentimentality is often reflected in the eternal topics on 'spring' or 'autumn' whose intellectual content is often low level, banal and repetitive. Geographers have long complained that the teaching about life in other countries is frequently dated and inaccurate, depicting people in clothing no longer worn or ignoring the rapid movement towards urban and industrial life which has taken place. Although most primary schools are in towns or suburbs there seems to be almost a conspiracy to pretend that life is still rural.

Bruner's project MACOS gave a sharp jolt to this unchallenged sentimentality when it depicted Eskimo life in all its harshness and brutality; so much so, that teachers became anxious about the emotional shock which children would receive from the bloody seal-hunting and the treatment of the elderly.

There is, however, a genuine problem for teachers with reference to 'sensitive issues' in the primary school. Different people have adopted different policies in this area. The team who planned *Social Studies 8-13* decided not to examine the family as an example of a human group because it might prove a 'sensitive' topic, but Hilda Taba devised a substantial sequence of lessons for six-year-olds on that subject, apparently without encountering difficulty. We have met teachers who thought it dangerous to suggest to children that all adults did not have unlimited authority and were therefore nervous about asking questions about the limits of an individual's power, e.g. Can the lollipop lady send you to bed early? Can a policeman send you to prison? This seems to us unduly authoritarian. We ourselves have however expressed doubts about the wisdom of a topic on race relations in this country. Another difficult subject is that of war. Children are easily interested in stories about World War 2 and what life was like then, when children were evacuated from their homes, a great adventure. Would we be prepared to read to them the diary of Anne Frank and explain its context? And is the nature of nuclear war a fit subject for discussion in a primary school when children are already interested in and well informed about rockets and space travel?

Our own conclusion would be that our wish to protect children from the uglier realities of the adult world should not lead us to misrepresent it, so that children have to unlearn in the secondary stage what they learned in the primary school. While we would not set out to confront the consequences of nuclear war in the classroom, we would not refuse to answer questions about it nor brush them aside.

To sum up, there is a small number of attitudes — such as favourable attitudes to schooling — which we would all agree are desirable. Beyond these, when we approach attitudes to social relationships, race, class, sex and the like, the question of whether to seek to influence children's attitudes in a particular direction is one for the individual conscience of the teacher. If, however, we do set out to influence attitudes then we must analyse, plan and evaluate just as rigorously as in the cognitive area. It is also worth remembering that, whatever we decide about trying to influence children's attitudes in sensitive areas, they will form such attitudes none the less.

Moral Education

Moral issues are involved in any field of the curriculum that considers human behaviour. They cannot therefore be treated as belonging solely to the content of religious education. Moral education may be regarded as essentially social: Kohlberg suggests it arises initially in children's attempts to grapple with the moral dilemmas springing from their experience of life in the human group, in the family, in the peer group and in the community. Topic work therefore, in so far as it deals with aspects of human life in these and other groups, must confront moral issues. It does so, for example, in the context of the topic we later outline on 'Desert Island' where we use the story of a boy who, chosen as a leader, abuses his authority. No doubt looking through the examples we use you will find a number of similar moral problems.

In this context we should perhaps make plain our position that, while there is undoubtedly an attitude component in moral development, since people may be able to understand a moral principle without being willing to act upon it, our concern with moral growth is in this area of the curriculum mainly cognitive. Empathy, the capacity to enter into the feelings of other people, is itself at least partly a cognitive process which can be initiated by questions such as 'What do you think X felt when he did this?' 'Why do you think he felt like that?' 'Have you ever felt like that?' etc.

In stressing the cognitive aspect of moral development we are in good company with Piaget and Kohlberg who both treat moral development in this way. They have both identified stages in the process of moral development ranging (in Piaget's case) from a pre-moral stage where the child's moral judgements are made in terms of the pleasant or unpleasant outcome of the action; a second stage where moral judgements are justified by reference to authority ('It's wrong because Miss Smith said so'); a third stage which stresses reciprocity ('I wouldn't like someone to do it to me'); a final stage of autonomy where the individual in making judgements is able to make allowances for motive and circumstances. Successors to Piaget like Kohlberg have modified the idea of developmental stages but, more important, have shown that progress through the stages may be accelerated and that the further up the ladder the child goes during his school days, the greater the chance of his moral development continuing in adult life. Happily too a strong correlation is found between the ability to make moral judgements and the practice of acting upon moral principle.

Our central concern then is, if progress in moral development can be accelerated, exactly how may this be done in the context of topic work? The first step is to identify the level at which children are operating, not we would suggest, so that we can slot them in to one of Piaget's or Kohlberg's stages, but so that we can consider 'which way is up', i.e. what can be done to advance understanding. To give an example: if a child says 'You shouldn't run down the corridor, Miss Smith says so', he is operating at a pretty low level. If we ask 'What happens if you do run down the corridor', he may say 'Miss X will be cross', 'What else may happen?' — 'Someone might get knocked down', we are then arriving at the understanding that rules are not arbitrary but made for reasons; a considerable advance. The next step up this ladder might involve the understanding that in some circumstances, rules are necessarily broken. Leaving corridor-running we might find an instance where rules are occasionally and in special circumstances ignored, in a study of the rules of the road, with which children are reasonably familiar. 'Which vehicles may break the speed limit and drive through traffic lights when they are red?' The children who are familiar with the dramatic movements of ambulances and fire engines may be brought to the understanding that saving human life may be a justification for breaking the law which exists to protect human life. Consequently quite young children may begin to grapple with the notion that the judgements we make depend on circumstances.

Consider, however, the following dialogue between a student teacher and her nine-year-old class after she had told the story of how, in the early nineteenth century, a little girl had been sent to prison for stealing a penny.

Teacher: Wasn't that awful, sending a little girl your age to jail?
Child A: She was stealing.

Teacher:	Yes, but wasn't sending her to jail cruel?
Child A:	Not to jail, but she was stealing.
Child B:	She has to be punished . . .
Child C:	Not jail, but could they have branded her?
Child B:	Brand her on her hand so people would know . . .?
Child D:	Cut her hand off. (laughter)
Teacher:	But she was starving!
Child C:	Well, they could give her food, some food, just a bit, and brand her and let her go.

Here the teacher was expecting the children to show a very subtle mixture of attitudes and opinions. They were not to approve of stealing but they were to make allowances for the child's motive in doing so. They were not to approve of the early-nineteenth century authorities' treatment of children as fully responsible for their actions, though the children had no doubt been constantly told that they themselves were responsible for what they did. They were expected to understand that punishment should relate to the seriousness of the offence. And they were to empathise with the starving child, although they themselves had probably never been more than mildly hungry and had always had almost unlimited access to food. All of this was too much. They had been taught to reject theft and expected approval for doing so. And their experience of history stories had probably led them to expect that such stories would be liberally laced with violence – and branding with a letter T for thief seemed appropriate to the period.

Given such a response what can we do? Clearly it would be unhelpful to pursue this particular issue in that session: there is no point in merely inviting children to be censorious. In the context of 'Desert Island' we did not ask the children how they would punish the boy who abused his responsibilities of leadership, but what, in the context of the peer group, they could do i.e. persuade him to change his ways, choose another leader, or go away and form a group without him. Further, the context of the story of the child and the penny is obviously too remote from the nine-year-old's experience. If we wish to raise their level of understanding we need to return to their moral world and find problems within it. For example, the children are familiar with the problem of accidental as opposed to deliberate damage as the cry 'I didn't mean to do it' frequently demonstrates. This involves the vital idea of making allowances for motive and intention and so, if we tell the story of a football accidentally kicked through a window, they may well be able to make a moral distinction between the action of the child who did not intend to break the glass and that of the vandal who did intend to do so. And if we wish to make the problem more subtle and more difficult we may say 'Suppose John and Jane decided to play near the greenhouse and knew that the ball was very likely to get kicked through the glass. Are they to blame if it is broken . . .?'

The subject of justice and law may provide similar opportunities. We know that six-year-olds often form their views of both from television and, if asked to draw pictures of policemen, show them with guns catching the baddies and putting them in prison. At the same time their day-to-day experience of rules and law is often formed by the instruction their mothers give about crossing roads and by their general experience of travel. They know for example there is a 70 mph speed limit on motorways though, said one, 'My daddy always goes at 80'. It is not difficult by questions such as 'What would happen if there were no traffic lights? What would happen if people parked cars where they liked?' to promote the idea that common wellbeing depends on respect for law. It does not require the teacher to take up a highly didactic stance to establish this understanding which is relevant to their moral progress.

Moral Education – Exercises

Can you think of homely, familiar problems which could be used to get children to consider the key moral idea that circumstances and motives legitimately affect our judgement of people's actions? Here is an example in the context of a topic about football:

> John is the captain of the football team and has to pick a team for the match against class 3. He decides he must leave Clive out of the team because he is no good. What does he say to Clive? Does he say 'You're out because you're no good' or does he say 'Well, Clive, you did quite well in the practice but I think I ought to try Jack out this week and give him a chance to show what he can do'. Here the moral problem is whether or not to tell the truth even if it is going to hurt someone's feelings.

(1) Now try to find another context for the same moral problem and write a little story about it ending with some question or task for the children.
(2) Then try to think up a context and a little story for another moral problem involving the inflicting of pain, i.e. in what circumstances is it right to hurt someone else and in what circumstances

wrong?

(3) Finally do the same thing using generosity as the issue. Is it always right to be generous?

Notes on Exercises

Moral Education Exercise 2

(2) Example of story about inflicting pain

Jane's mother is very cross with her for teasing the cat. Jane has dressed the cat up in dolls' clothes and the cat is miserable. Jane made things worse by trying to pin the clothes on and in doing so stuck the pin into the cat. The cat howls with pain. Jane's mother says 'Stop that Jane. You are really hurting Puss. It's cruel.' The next day Puss is limping badly. Jane's mother finds he has something stuck in his paw. They decide to take him to the vet and put him into a basket. He hates this and howls worse than ever. At the vet's, the vet removes the thorn but obviously hurts the cat, as much as Jane had hurt him in her play. Jane says to her mother 'Wasn't the vet cruel?' What does her mother say, do you think? Is there any difference between the way Jane hurt the cat and the way the vet did so?

PART TWO

RESOURCES FOR LEARNING

4 PICTURES

Every teacher realises that learners — adults as well as children — are able to cope with a new area of study with greater confidence, speed and likelihood of success if they are provided with what the educational psychologist refers to as 'concrete' support for the thinking involved. Whilst it is certainly true that one of the criteria on which cognitive development might be assessed is the increasing independence of such concrete support for the mental manipulation of concepts and propositions, we all seek recourse to examples and models as an aid to understanding and reasoning and it must, just as certainly, be part of the teacher's role to provide such concrete support and provide for his pupils to make the best possible use of it. For example, no teacher would expect his pupils to develop a concept of length from a purely symbolic exposition about linear distance and standardised units. Over a fairly lengthy period the teacher would provide for the child to handle material and to see examples whilst at the same time using appropriate vocabulary such as 'long', 'short', 'longer than', 'shorter than'. From there the child might go on to ordering three or more pieces of material in terms of their length, start to compare materials of different length against some arbitrary units such as his hand or a book before proceeding to use and handle standardised units and, at the same time, talking about them in a great many different situations. Later on the child will usually be capable of understanding and working on propositions which refer to matters of linear measurement and to units of measure such as the metre, without direct reference and recourse to concrete models and examples; but it is a fairly slow process.

Such direct experience is invaluable in all conceptual development. A child's understanding of the concept of change is likely to be more effectively developed if he has experienced some change in his own life and has thought about it. If he has moved house he will be able to list the similarities and differences between the two houses and their situations, he is likely to know about at least one possible reason for change — his father getting a new job or being promoted for example — he is better able to make judgements about what is good about change (a bigger house, bigger garden) and what is not so good (losing contact with friends, greater distance from the shops or school) and perhaps get some deeper understanding of how peoples' values change with their circumstances. His grasp then of the causes and effects of change and so of the concept of change itself will be developed more efficiently through his experience than through any system of his having to listen to teacher exposition or having to read about it in the abstract.

Teachers can, of course, make use of such experience and help to provide it and subsequent chapters in this book deal with both the use of the child's day-to-day experience and such teacher-sponsored experiences as visits.

However, neither opportunity nor time allow for every idea we want to introduce to children to be accompanied by direct experience and indeed vicarious experiences can often be just as useful. One form of vicarious experience which has traditionally been available to teachers comes in the form of pictures and one would include under this heading maps, diagrams and graphs. Such material is certainly not in short supply, and the popular educational press provides a great variety of pictures so that most schools and many individual teachers have a vast stock upon which to draw.

Whilst pictures are, of course, useful as a means of supplying incidental background information when they are displayed on classroom walls or as a means of attracting children towards a classroom display, they also form an invaluable classroom resource for cognitive development. In this latter context, however, they are frequently neglected and yet they are really of far more use to the teacher in the primary school than many books, for at least three reasons. In the first place there is a much greater variety of subject content suitable for topic work in pictures than there are available books; secondly, pictures provide — through the examples and models they illustrate — concrete support for the ideas embedded in them which the words of a sentence or passage in a book do not provide; and thirdly, questions can be set on a picture without the danger that the child will be able to copy or paraphrase as he can from a book in giving his answer. In addition pictures have an obvious advantage in any situation where there are children of limited literacy.

This section deals with the kinds of questions that might be asked using pictures. Questions should, of course, always be designed to promote thinking rather than simple recall. For example, if we refer back to the child who moved house the question 'What time did the removal van arrive?' promotes little thought — the child simply has to remember. The question 'Why do most people hire a removal van when they move house?' gets the child into thinking about specialisation, efficiency, expertise, convenience and similar ideas if he is to give an adequate answer. Concept formation depends upon the child being asked to think about an idea in as many different ways as possible and to use that idea in the largest possible number of ways and situations. This matter of thinking about an idea — at a higher level than simple recall — is essential if the child is to grasp the idea and develop his understanding of it. We can help children to develop concepts then by getting them to apply a range of thinking strategies or thinking skills to the ideas or concepts we want them to develop.

There are several lists of these skills — often referred to in the literature as intellectual skills — with similar thinking processes being given different names. This book uses those thinking processes listed in Bloom's taxonomy as the basis for the categorisation of questions and tasks that follow. What is important, however, is that teachers acquire a serviceable and comprehensible check list of intellectual skills and a full understanding of the kind of tasks, by questions for their pupils, which will develop those skills. The list of intellectual skills suggested in this chapter and developed elsewhere in this book is fairly short and simple and can no doubt be added to, revised or re-organised in the light of further reading or experience. What is important at this stage is that teachers realise that asking questions is not an unstructured, random exercise — the principle of specific question types must be borne in mind and applied to oral question/answer and discussion sessions, to the making of work-cards and similar task-setting procedures.

Before we look at the various categories of questions in relation to pictures, it might be useful to emphasise that not all pictures are equally suitable for use as a basis for questions and task-setting, and it is a matter of some importance if the session is to be a success that the pictures selected are carefully chosen. The best pictures will be those full of activity. If we want to question children about the role of the police in our society so as to develop their understanding of such concepts as authority, or law, or rules, or interdependence or such, then a picture could be very useful. However, a picture of a policeman standing to attention in front of a static background of houses would be of little use. The picture most useful here would be one showing a range of police activities. The policeman might be stopping the traffic in a busy street, interviewing passers-by or others involved in an accident, using dogs to find evidence, speaking on his two-way radio and similar activities.

In such pictures will be a wide range of visual clues, which will provide children with the kind of help they may need to answer questions about the role of the police, the reasons why such a role is necessary in society, the possible effects of not having a police force on individuals and on society as a whole. But using pictures and finding the clues as a means of answering questions and solving problems has to be taught and developed over a long period and is the basis of intellectual skill acquisition.

Pictures are especially useful in the development of four of these intellectual skills – interpretation, classification, extrapolation and evaluation. The interpretation of a picture involves explaining what the picture is communicating to an observer. It involves giving reasons for the things observed and making deductions and inferences. The child has to be taught to recognise and interpret the symbols that will indicate, for example, status – 'Which of the men in the picture is in charge?' or 'Are the people in the picture slaves or freemen?' The pictorial symbols will also give clues as to the reasons for things – for example, 'Why does the miner in the picture wear a helmet?' or 'Why do you think the castle walls are so high?' Interpretation questions frequently, though not always of course, begin with what? or how? or why?

'What are the people in the picture doing?'
'How do you know the man in the picture is a policeman?'
'Why do you think the birds in the picture have such long legs?'
'What are the houses in the picture made of?'
'Have the people in the picture any enemies?'
'How do the people in the picture get their food?'
'What are the tools made of?'

Pictures will not, of course, always be used in isolation and will usually only be one source of information simultaneously available to the children as a means of developing concepts and generalisations. For example a topic on the Lapps may have as one of its intentions the development of the concept of culture or way of life and in particular the idea of a nomadic culture. Part of understanding this concept will be the realisation that there are specific reasons why a group of people like the Lapps spend their lives moving about from place to place. It will be necessary to grasp the notion that this movement is not random but to do with food and water supply, with the movement of reindeer herds and the availability of pasture. Understanding will need to be developed not only of the causes but also of the effects of such a way of life in terms of the kind of shelter such people built, the skills they developed and the values they held. What is important here is not simply the understanding of the idea of culture in the context of the Lapps and understanding the cause and effects of such a life style on their behaviour. What is of even more value is that the child is now better able to transpose and extend the idea from the Lapps to, say, the Bedouin Arab. A child who has understood nomadic in the context of Laplanders ought to be able to infer, hypothesise, generalise about the environment the Bedouin lives in and indicate, as an instance, the kind of shelter he is likely to build, given the one piece of information 'Bedouin Arabs are nomads'. Working for this kind of understanding and ability requires that our questions tease out the causes and effects of, in this case, being a nomad.

So, if we used picture A as the basis of a discussion or on a work-card we might ask the following interpretation questions:

(1) What is happening in the picture?
(2) Why is the Laplander lassoing the reindeer?
(3) Why have they brought a sled with them?
(4) What do you think the Lapps use to make their tents?

Picture A

At the same time, other information available through books or stories will allow a further range of complementary interpretation questions to be asked:

(1) Why do you think the nomadic Lapps live in tents and not houses?
(2) What do you think the nomadic Lapps make their clothes of. Why are they so decorative?

(3) Why do they find dogs so useful when they are hunting the
    reindeer?

There are other interpretation questions that could be asked on this
picture but those listed are probing the ideas that the nomadic Lapps
need to hunt for their food supply, that they have easily transportable
belongings (a tent for example) and have devised efficient ways of
carrying their goods — all matters to do with their particular lifestyle
or culture.

Picture B, on the other hand, helps to develop the idea of cultural
change and to investigate the causes and effects of that change in terms
of a new lifestyle, new ways of providing the necessities of life and the
skills required of a settled farmer as against a nomadic hunter. The
following interpretation question might be asked on picture B.

(1) Why has the Laplander built a house and put up fences?
(2) What do you think he is doing?
(3) Do you think the reindeer will try to escape?

Picture B

log house

Exercise 1

Devise a number of interpretation questions on picture C. Try to relate
your questions to some particular idea(s) you are seeking to develop.

Classification can also be taught through the use of pictures. The ability to classify phenomena is of vital importance in the extension of conceptual understanding. Classification requires a child to seek for the characteristic criteria that will allow them to place phenomena into the correct pigeonhole. Being able to place a new piece of phenomena into its correct pigeonhole in this way prevents the confusion that would be perpetually with us if every new situation we met was unique. The fact that the world is not so confusing as that is because we have this sorting arrangement to help us organise the mass of incoming information.

Picture C

We develop the ability to classify by providing for children to list items under various headings. Which heading they put a particular item under will depend on their being able to identify common characteristics of all the items under the same heading. Later on they will recognise the possibility that some items may go under more than one heading and will be able to label groups of items themselves. An aspect of this skill is often referred to as application, by which we mean that the child is able to apply his understanding about a particular grouping to a new situation when we ask him the question 'Is the man in the picture holding a weapon or a tool?' Here the child has to apply his knowledge about the characteristics of a weapon and of a tool to the new phenomena and so put it into the correct pigeonhole. Of course it may be the child could answer 'Well on the one hand it is designed as a tool for chopping down trees and cutting the trunks into pieces suitable for building the boat which is being made in the picture but he could use it as a weapon if he were attacked because it has a sharp metal head and a long shaft . . .' However getting such tentativeness into a child's answer may take a very long time.

Classification/application questions on pictures help children then to a better grasp of a concept and an extension of that grasp or understanding. By this is meant not only knowing more instances of what fits into that particular conceptual group, but also knowing that examples of a concept or grouped items can often appear to be superficially quite different. Examples of such questions are:

(1) Which people in the picture are working?
(2) Which building in the picture are factories?
(3) How many different jobs are being done in the picture?
(4) How many forms of defence can be seen in the picture?
(5) Which of the animals are reptiles?
(6) How many different kinds of transport can you see in the picture?
(7) Which of the people in the picture are rich and which are poor?

Exercise 2

Devise classification questions on pictures A, B and C.

A third skill we can develop using pictures is the skill of evaluation. Primary schools have been criticised in the past for failing to require children to make judgements or to express their opinions. Children can be encouraged to evaluate information through the process of offering opinions about it. To do this they must balance some aspects of the information they are receiving against other aspects and perhaps to come up with reasons both for and against the idea they are being asked to make a judgement about. The child, who in answer to the question 'Would you like to live in a cave?' asked in the context of some topic work on cavemen, comes up with the answer 'Yes, if the cave were dry; some were not. You could defend the entrance of it if it was not too wide. Not if it were wet. It would be cold' has already got the idea of giving arguments pro and con and of giving reasons for his views.

On the Lapp picture A we can ask evaluation questions such as 'Is the sled a good way of carrying things?' and 'Would dogs be most useful to nomadic Lapps who hunt reindeer or settled Lapps who own farms?' and, in the same context, questions like 'Would you like to be a nomad like the Lapps in picture A?' 'Who would have the hardest life, a nomadic Lapp or a settled Lapp?'

All these questions ask the children to weigh up the evidence and express an opinion about the things we want the children to understand — what culture is and how it is affected by environmental and other factors.

Other examples of evaluation questions might be:

(1) Look at the picture (or the map) and say which is the best place to cross the road.
(2) Which warriors have the best weapons?
(3) Is red a good colour for a fire engine?
(4) Are modern tools better than the tools you can see in the picture?
(5) Is the village in the picture easy to defend?

Exercise 3

Look at picture D. This is an excellent example of the kind of picture that lends itself to the asking of a large variety of questions about worthwhile ideas or concepts, for example trade, defence and environment. Write down as many questions as you can based on this picture under the three headings we have considered so far — interpretation, classification (application) and evaluation.

We can also ask children to use their understanding of a concept to go well beyond the information they have and to determine the implications, consequences and effects of some change or extension of that information. This is called extrapolation and is yet another intellectual skill that we can foster using pictures. We are asking the child to forecast how a situation he can see in the picture might develop and will require him to use and extend his thinking about such important ideas as cause and effect. 'What do you think will happen next in the picture?' is a useful extrapolation question on a picture, especially when the picture being used is one which implies action. Other examples of questions are:

(1) How would the lives of the people in the picture be changed if the

weather got colder?

(2) What will happen if the flood water in the picture gets any higher?

(3) What might happen if the lollipop lady did not have a uniform?

(4) (using picture B) 'How will the farming Lapp feed his reindeer in the winter?

(5) (using picture D) 'What will happen if the people cannot agree about what is a fair exchange?

Picture D

In setting questions on pictures or in any other context it is of course quite unnecessary to keep the different categories separate. On picture D we could reasonably ask:

(1) What has each group brought to trade with? (interpretation)

(2) What do you think will happen next? (extrapolation)

(3) Why do you think the groups need the goods they will receive? (interpretation)

Indeed the sequence of question 'What is happening?' 'What will happen next?' 'Why?' is both natural and logical.

There are other intellectual skills or thinking strategies which are dealt with elsewhere in this book. It is particularly important that teachers deliberately aim to foster such strategies in their pupils if conceptual understanding is to develop, since understanding only comes through looking at and thinking about information from a variety of different points of view.

For example, if we want children to understand the concept of social change it is not simply a matter of telling them that things are no longer the same as before. We would need to get the children at the appropriate level to list the changes they can find evidence of and to think about the reasons why such changes took place; to classify and categorise examples of change according to its probable or identified cause, to evaluate the benefits or disadvantages of change, and to hypothesise about the consequences of lack of change or of different kinds of change of which there is no direct evidence.

Of course once we have started asking such questions and got children to start thinking in appropriate ways we need to gently improve the quality of their answers. This means the teacher thinking out the answers to his own questions and deciding what will be a good evaluation or interpretation answer and what will be a poor one. Failure to do this will result in the teacher missing opportunities to improve the quality of the child's answer through clues and prompts.

Generally an answer will be better if:

(a) the number of possibilities considered is increased;
(b) there is a suggestion of tentativeness about any conclusions.

This progress in thinking ability does not develop spontaneously. It must be taught just as the skills themselves must be. The following questions asked about picture D are answered at three different levels of quality. The first level is the acceptable minimum and the second and third levels indicate an improvement in quality in the ways suggested above. It would be useful for the reader to consider what he might say to a child who gave the minimum answer, by way of prompts and clues, to get that child to supply an answer nearer to the second or third stages.

Interpretation
Q: What are the group of men doing?

A: (1) Talking to each other.
      (2) Talking to each other about trading and trying to decide how
          much the tools are worth.
      (3) They are trading tools for jewellery. The traders are probably
          eager to get the tools and so may have to be the ones who
          give way on the amount of each to be swapped.

Extrapolation

Q: What will happen if they cannot agree?
A: (1) They will fight.
      (2) They will fight and the trading will come to an end and the
          traders won't get any tools.
      (3) The trading will stop but probably only for a while because
          the traders need tools much more than the village people
          need jewellery so it is likely they will back down.

Application/Classification

Q: Is this a primitive community?
A: (1) Yes they wear skins.
      (2) Yes they wear skins and live in huts and they haven't any
          money.
      (3) They do have primitive tools and boats but on the other hand
          they are well organised as a community and in matters of
          trade and defence — so they are not all that primitive.

Evaluation

Q: Is this an efficient (or good) way to trade?
A: (1) No, the village people may not want jewellery.
      (2) No. They might not want each others' goods and in any case
          it would be hard to agree on how many axes for a necklace.
      (3) Well it isn't as good as having money because the things are
          quite big — but if amber is rare, small bits could be quite
          valuable and at least it is portable and a bit like money.

Like most kinds of progress this development of thinking abilities will
not come overnight but it will come if it is part of the teacher's
questioning technique to provide for it.

Exercise 4

Take the questions already devised in Exercises 1, 2 and 3. Answer each
question at three levels indicating:

(a) an answer you would accept but at the minimum level of quality;

(b) the answer improved by the inclusion of more considered possibilities,

(c) the answer improved by an indication of the tentative nature of these possibilities.

5 BOOKS

When we come to consider the use of books in topic work, we must first be aware of three important intellectual skills which come into their own most strongly when we are dealing with the written word. The first of these is what Bloom calls 'translation from one level of abstraction to another'. What this rather forbidding formula involves is simply this, if we ask a child to put in his own words what 'barter' means, or if we say 'It says in the book that Mr Jones is the manager of the dairy — what does a "manager" do?', then we are asking the child to 'translate'.

This activity of 'translating' has two values. One is obvious, it is an essential testing device, in that if the children do not understand the concepts 'barter' or 'manager', they cannot 'put them into their own words'. Secondly, and less obviously, the act of 'translating' itself serves to clarify and strengthen a child's grasp of a concept, as in this oral 'translation' of 'barter'.

> Its like giving things, so, if I give somebody, er, some budgie seed and they swopped me some marbles. Not money. Like budgie seed for marbles.

The child here first tries the idea of 'giving', then retracts it. Then she casts about for an example of something one could barter with and comes up with 'budgie seed'. This forcing of the learner to provide their own illustrative examples is one of the more valuable aspects of 'translation', in that an example taken from your own store of interest and experience — i.e. 'budgie seed' — is likely to be more lively and memorable than one offered you by an outsider. Finally she crystallises the idea in five words 'Like budgie seed for marbles', having on the way dismissed the idea of money. For further illustration of the value of this exercise, you could try writing down clear explanations, without using dictionaries, of some high level abstraction like 'Common Market', 'imperialism' or 'primitive' and see whether your own understanding is enhanced by the effort of 'translating' the idea into simpler terms.

Translation need not involve only words-to-words, as it were. It is equally legitimate to ask a child to translate some idea like 'raid' 'farm' or 'factory' into a drawing, and we will later pursue further this form of translating.

There are two further skills which complete our repertoire: synthesis and analysis. Synthesis is involved whenever a child composes a response to some task or question requiring more than one or two words; it is the organising of words (or pictures) into the most appropriate and effective order. Its importance runs far beyond the topic area, it is improved by frequent practice and by force of example and all teachers are very well aware of its importance, whatever name they may use for it.

Analysis is equally vital as a skill, it could in fact be called the key to all other skills, because it involves, simply, knowing what to do, what skills to use, when faced with a task. As educated adults, we are very adept at analysis. When, in an exam situation, we read on the paper 'Discuss the view that joining the EEC has been a disaster for Britain', we know the following things: (i) we are required to *write* an answer (not, as the word 'discuss' seems to imply, talk to our neighbour in the next desk about it); (ii) we are required to write quite a lot, probably about a thousand words or more; (iii) we are supposed to say something on both sides of the question; (iv) we will be rewarded if we can quote statistics or things important people have said about this question; (v) we must write in a formal, non-conversational way. We know all this, and more, even though we may not have the faintest idea how to answer the actual question itself.

Unfortunately, we are also prone to forget that we were not born knowing these things, and that when we ask children to 'Find out about', or 'Write about . . .' or 'Write a story about . . .' their success will depend heavily on knowing the conventions involved in 'Finding out . . .' etc. In other words, before a child can evaluate, extrapolate, translate or whatever, the child must know that that is what is required, must *analyse* the task, in fact. Look at the following two stories about 'The Cavemen Find a new Way of Living'.

A. (Sarah) We all decided that the cave was no good any more a place to live so we went to the forest. We tried to make houses out from wood and it was very hard and they leaked in the rain then our chief had a good idea and we put mud and leaves in the cracks to keep the rain out so we had nice new huts for houses.
B. (Carl) Our tribe has a new place to live. It is in the forest in the trees our chief took us their one day and we all waked down their to our new place to live. We will be happy in our new place. There are trees and rocks and a river.

Sarah has *interpreted* the move ('no good any more a place to live'), *extrapolated* successfully by anticipating the difficulties of making timber huts and the solution to the difficulty, and *synthesised* the whole thing into a fair narrative.

Carl has also synthesised quite well, so he is obviously not illiterate, but his account is absolutely banal because he has not addressed the questions of 'Why move?' and 'What problems might arise?' as Sarah has. In other words, he has not analysed the task 'Write a story called "The Cavemen Find a new Way of Living" ' adequately. We cannot know how he would have responded if he had been asked, instead of 'Write a story . . .', 'Why do you think the cavemen might have moved to the forest?' 'What problems might they have had making houses in the forest?'

The moral is that we must both find a place for the tightly structured tasks which do most of the 'analysing' for the child, and also for broader tasks where the child must analyse the task into its parts, as Sarah has done. However, before we see how this particular skill of analysis, and indeed, all the other intellectual skills, might be approached through books, we must ask ourselves the more general question — what is the function of books in topic work?

Tony is doing a topic on 'building' and is using the little book on *Building* in the excellent Macdonald 'First Library' series. He has been set the task 'find out about masons', and he has correctly used the index which refers to page 5. Page 5 reads as follows: 'The pyramids were built of stone. The stones were carried on wooden sledges. Hundreds of men pulled the stones up ramps. The ramps went round and round the pyramid. Masons cut the stones to fit in place. The tomb was built right in the middle of the pyramid.' Tony writes down 'Masons cut the stones to fit in place' and then moves on to do the next task on the work-card.

This little transaction is probably typical of thousands of such uses of book-text made by thousands of children in our schools every day. Many teachers would defend the value of what Tony did on the grounds that he was 'learning how to learn', that using the index correctly, and finding the appropriate line on page 5 were processes of value in themselves, transferable to thousands of future situations in which Tony might want to learn something for himself from a book. Taken to extremes, this approach places little if any emphasis on the actual information itself, and stresses the 'learning to learn' process as the supreme goal of 'topic' work involving the use of books.

Many other teachers, however, would feel disquiet about Tony's efforts, and they would be right to do so. In the first place, although the correct use of the index is obviously admirable, the task set for Tony represents a very inadequate view of what is involved in using a book or books to learn things from.

Suppose an adult heard that his son or daughter was going to live and work in Colombo, knew nothing of Colombo except that it was in southern Asia and wanted to know more, then he might look up 'Colombo' in, say, *Encyclopaedia Britannica*. There, he would meet the following first sentence of a short account of Colombo: 'Colombo, the capital and principal seaport of Ceylon, lies on the west coast of the island just south of the mouth of the Kelani River.' It is extremely unlikely that he would write that sentence down verbatim as Tony did. What he *would* do is start to use the information, relating it to concepts he already possesses: 'Capital — well, there should be a bit of entertainment — probably other British people living there — coast — should get some swimming and sailing if the beaches are decent.' He might, of course, make notes on the rest of the article if he had some need to fix the information (perhaps to pass on to other members of the family). In that case, the notes would probably look something like: 'Capital — quite big — seaside — hot — lots of rain — daily air-services.' Whether notes were made or not, however, the whole operation of information seeking (apart from the initial use of an index to find the information) would have virtually nothing in common with Tony's approach to the question of masons.

A second, major objection to the style of work that Tony has been set to do, is that it is very difficult to evaluate. Does Tony understand what he has copied down? Would he have copied down equally happily 'The masons drop the slargs over the tems', or some other account of masons which would be as meaningless to him as slargs and tems are to us? A boy of ten, of good intelligence and all round ability had just copied down from a book the sentence 'Thrushes like to eat snails', and moved on to his next task (copying a picture of a thrush). Less than a minute later a visitor to the classroom engaged him in conversation about his work and asked 'Do you know what thrushes eat?' The boy replied 'No'. When the visitor pointed out, very casually, that there seemed to be something in the boy's topic-book about thrushes eating things, the boy said 'Oh, oh yes — it says thrushes like to eat snails'. Is Tony operating at this sort of purely mechanical level, like someone transcribing things in an unknown foreign language? None of these questions can be confidently answered unless we question Tony privately, which takes away most of the operational value of having books in the classroom at all, i.e. the possibilities they create of letting children work independently, with minimum supervision for relatively long periods.

Some of these objections to this style of work can be partly met by teaching children to paraphrase, or 'use their own words'. 'Masons were men that cut the stones to fit in place' as a response certainly gives us a bit more confidence that the child has actually comprehended the text, but what of these paraphrases?

(a) 'Masons cut the stones and fit the place.'
(b) 'Masons cut some stones to fit the tomb.'
(c) 'Masons cutted the stones to fit in place.'

(a) and (b) may or may not show important misunderstandings, or they may be, as (c) clearly appears to be, just desperate attempts to make some kind of change in what is already a perfectly satisfactory piece of clear and simple prose. Many children find this business of 'putting things in their own words' very difficult, and a great deal of energy is misdirected into merely rephrasing prose which was perfectly well phrased in the first place.

The real criticism to be mounted against the task that Tony was set, though, is a positive not a negative one. This very short passage on pyramids (leaving aside the picture which accompanies it) allows major opportunities for concept development and the exercises of thinking skills, opportunities which are neglected by the 'Find out about . . .' approach. If, for example, the masons do *not* cut the stones to fit in place, or do it badly, the whole structure might fall down, and the labours of the 'hundreds of men' pulling stones up ramps, might be wasted. That being so, it seems reasonable that learning to be a mason would take quite a time, at least compared with learning to pull stones up ramps. It also might well be that a mason's rewards by way of pay, or, if he were a slave, good treatment, better food and the like, would be greater than those of a puller of stones. In other words this very small piece of text allows for the investigation of the concept of a 'skilled' man, his training, his responsibilities, his status. Specific questions involving intellectual skills that might be asked, to illuminate this concept could include:

(a) What might happen if the masons cut the stones wrongly?
    (extrapolation)
(b) Were masons more important than the other workers? (evaluation)
(c) Would it be fair if the masons got more money or food than the

other workers? (evaluation)
(d) How do you think the masons learned their job? (interpretation)
(e) Can you think of some other jobs that take a long time to learn?
(classification)

Provided that children have learned to move beyond the stage of
'yes-no' answers to questions like (b) and (c), their responses to tasks
like this will give us a fairly clear view of their level of understanding of
masons as skilled men, since they will be unavoidably engaged in
thinking about the question as well as using the index, reading and
writing.

This approach also provides us with an answer to two questions of
fundamental importance about books and their place in topic-work:
what are books for, and what makes one book better for our purposes
than another? The prose on page 5 of *Building* could have been written
by any teacher — it contains no out-of-the-way information, and is
unremarkable in style. However, it is very cunningly wrought. It sets
us up to do useful work on masons as skilled workers, and it also
allows us, if we wish, to start investigating the differences between
primitive technology ('Hundreds of men pulled the stones . . .') and
technology today and also the idea of a social and organisational
structure supporting ambitious public works (how would all these
'hundreds of men' be fed, and who would stop them running away?)
All this, in the space of 48 words, is there to be used if we want it.

The text of a good book, in other words, is a well-contrived springboard for learning, and it supplements the other springboards we use
— pictures, the children's own experience, and our own ingenuity and
imagination in devising materials and situations to promote learning.
The basic test of a 'good' book then (leaving aside for the moment the
question of matching the readability of the text to the children's actual
reading ability) is not so much 'what does it tell me?' but 'what can I
ask about it?'

From this point of view, we have to be particularly careful about
the danger of selecting attractive and informative books which, in fact,
close questions down, instead of opening them up. For example, page
5 of *Building* might have read: 'Masons were the most important
workers. They cut the stones to fit in place. If they did it wrong the
stones would not fit. They had a long training. They were better treated
than the other builders, because they were so skilful.' Most of our
original questions have been partly or wholly answered by the text in
this new form and we may or may not find it easy to devise new things

to ask. In this particular case, we might well ask a child to say in his own words (or 'translate') what 'better treatment' might mean, and 'translation' tasks like this are often possible to set, and useful, on the more elaborate and explanatory texts which tend to close up other possibilities. The actual, spare, text however, was clearly better for our purposes.

Even if a text lends itself well to use as a basis for concept and skill development through questions, we may still not get maximum value from it, unless we phrase our questions well. If we take page 23 of *Building*, we find the following text:

> In hot dry countries, houses are built to keep the heat out. The walls are thick and painted in pale colours. The windows are just big enough to let in light, but not let in heat. There is no glass in the windows so that breezes can cool the house.

Obviously, the important idea of environment affecting house-building styles is involved here, and we might be tempted to put some question like 'What are houses in hot, dry countries like?' If we put that question, however, we are very likely to get the contents of page 23 copied verbatim by way of an answer, because that is the most sensible response by any child seeking to give an accurate and complete reply. Unfortunately, the process may not have involved much thinking by the child and is, of course, very hard for us to evaluate. We must always check that the most sensible way to answer any of our questions is not, in fact, to copy out a section of the text. In the case of this particular text, to get children thinking, we might have to go to the idea that environmental pressures, especially severe ones, do not produce ideal houses, but compromises. Thus we might ask 'What would be the snags about living in houses like those it tells you about on page 23' or, more specifically, giving more clues:

> 'What would be the snag about having very small windows?'
> 'What would be the snag about having no glass in windows?'

If there are no questions that commend themselves on a given small piece of text, we might still use a page like 23 as part of some larger, looser exercise involving analysis, note-taking and summarising skills (see below, p. 72). But before we leave the question of basing questions closely on fairly small sections of text, we should look at some further examples.

Exercise 1

Decide in the case of each of the following short extracts:

(a) whether it is suitable as a basis for questions and tasks at all;
(b) if it is, what questions might be set on it, and what concept or
    concepts might be approached through those questions?

Extract A (*Building*, Macdonald 'First Library', 1973)
   Long ago, men did not build houses. They lived in caves. Later,
   men learned to build shelters from branches. In some countries
   people built huts of stone.

Extract B (*China Long Ago*, Macdonald 'Starters', 1972)
   The Chinese thought small feet were beautiful. They bandaged
   girls' feet to stop them growing. This hurt the girls when they
   walked.

Extract C (*A First Look at Cloth* by Robin Kerrod, Franklin Watts,
1973)
   Most of our clothes, of course, are produced in factories. They
   are made in a variety of standard sizes so that they can fit people
   of more or less any size, shape and build.
      These clothes are called *ready-to-wear* or *off-the-peg* clothes.
   But to get a perfect fit, you must go to a *tailor*. He takes your
   exact measurements and makes clothes specially for you. We call
   them *made-to-measure* clothes.

Extract D (*A First Look at the Post* by Valerie Pitt, Franklin Watts,
1973)
   For the very earliest mail-carriers, life was full of hazards. Long
   ago a Persian ruler set up his own postal system. He had a *relay
   team* of riders and horses, so his messages could be carried far across
   the land. His riders rode over deserts, through mountain ranges,
   across gushing rivers. Wild animals were on the prowl, robbers waited
   to waylay them.

Extract E (*A First Look at the Post*)
   Not all of *London's* mail goes to the railway station by van. Some
   of it travels underground on the *Post Office Railway*. Driverless
   trains, rushing along at 55 kilometres an hour, carry the mail below
   the streets of London — beating traffic jams, snow-storms and
   hold-ups.

Books can be used as the basis of many other activities, besides close
questioning on the ideas in short passages. In fact, obviously, the

technique of close questioning described above must be used quite sparingly — nobody wants to work through a whole book at the rate of half-a-page a day, however interesting and useful the tasks involved might be.

Note-taking

Reading fairly long stretches of text and making brief notes on the contents is a very useful learning technique. It is a very commonly used strategy in secondary schooling, though much less often used in the junior years, which is a pity.

The little book on *Building* with which we started this chapter would lend itself to the setting of a note-making task on these lines: 'Note down what people have made *houses* from, and what they have made important buildings from. Give the page numbers where you find things out. Make notes in two columns — I will give you a start, like this.

Houses		Important Buildings	
Branches	(page 1)	Pyramids — stone	(page 4)
Stone	(page 1)	Temples — stone	(page 6)
Mud	(page 2)		
Wood	(page 2)		

There are several important points about this task. First, it is important to check that the task will allow the child to find relevant material on most of the book or section's pages. The child has to learn that the art of note-taking involves knowing what to leave out, that, say, a whole page devoted to the detail of brick-making techniques has nothing to contribute to this particular task, and must be read carefully but nevertheless not intrude into the end-product notes. However, it is very dispiriting to read page after page of a book, only to find that the information is not relevant to your purpose, and if the task had referred only to 'important buildings', 13 pages out of 28 of this particular book would have been irrelevant. The task as set leaves only seven pages with nothing to contribute. This particular task can run right to the end of this particular book, but very commonly you will have to designate sections of the book as the basis of such tasks, rather than try to invent tasks which artificially unify material with several different themes.

Secondly, in this instance the child is given clear instructions, and examples as guides, on several important matters – how to lay out the notes, how much to write under each heading, how to give the page references. On the other hand, the child is left to work out alone the tactical problem of whether to read the whole book through looking at 'houses' and then at 'important buildings', or to try to run the note-taking in both columns simultaneously. The conceptual problem, of what constitutes an 'important building' is also left to the child to sort out. More guidance than this example offers would have to be given to children quite unaccustomed to making notes, and they will particularly require guidance and encouragement in leaving things out, but the target must be that the child makes gradually more and more of the decisions about how to take the present notes.

Thirdly, it is important that having taken the notes, we can do something with them. In this case, for example, we could ask the child to evaluate the pros and cons of the different materials used for home-building, and to classify the different sorts of 'important buildings', both tasks being performed not by reference to the book, but by reference to the notes. The notes, in other words, have become a learning resource, which is, after all, what notes are supposed to be.

Finally, it should be noted that this task, involving a whole book, is quite ambitious, especially, of course, for slow readers, but in fact, in the case of this particular book, a worthwhile note-making task on the same lines could have been set on the first eight pages, containing 317 words (including some picture-captions). Another important criterion for book-selection is suggested by all this, i.e. does the book in question have coherent themes, running for a reasonable number of consecutive pages, which can form the basis for some worthwhile exercises in note-making?

Imaginative Works – Synthesis

It is easy to forget, as we solemnly address the problems of note-making and task-setting, that many modern books for young children have been designed, both in text and through pictures, to be exciting, to stir imagination. The book quoted in extract B of Exercise 1, *China Long Ago* is a good case in point. Page 4 contains a very lively picture of a Mongol assault on the Great Wall, and the following text:

> The Mongols were fierce enemies of China. They attacked China even when the wall was built.

What this text and picture made Clive (9) want to do, was not answer questions, but write a story. He wrote as follows:

> We were all scared when the Mongols came at the wall but we got out bows and I got one then my friend right by me was killd by an arrow so I killd some more enemies for revenge. We soldiers drove (them) off and China was saved. Then they came back again and again with bows and arrows but we had our bows and arrows.

Clive was persuaded to have another shot at a Great Wall story, after having looked up (i) what Chinese soldiers wore (p. 5), (ii) how people got letters written (public letter writer, p. 24). This was the result:

> Dear dad I am getting the letter-writer to write to you about the battle. lots of us were killed but we killed more of (the) mongols and we had our big strongcloth uniforms like armor so we wernt so scard. My friend was killed and China was saved again I practise bow and arrow every day in case they come again.

The idea of revenge which gave some life to the first version has been lost from the second, but the whole account reads a bit more like a description of a battle in ancient China rather than a battle anywhere, anytime. The detail of the 'letter-writer' and the protective uniforms has come from guided reading of parts of the book, the evocative idea of daily archery practice 'in case they come again' may have come from the book, or from Clive's own head, him having been given time for reflection. Clive professed himself better pleased with version two, on the grounds that it was 'more exciting'.

When children are writing stories, as in this case, not from their own experience, but from second-hand experience (largely television) it is always worth getting them to spend time doing what an adult would do in like cases, research the background a bit, look for some local colour and evocative detail. The risk is that the child may go 'off the boil' as it were, and lose spontaneity. (Even very adult novelists can write things like 'I swiftly drew my seven-inch bronze dagger from its Sicilian boiled horse-hide sheath, its chased Minoan-style silver pommel-plate caught the moonlight as . . .' passages, which make us wish they had perhaps done a bit less research and given a little more attention to plot and character). The case of Clive suggests that this may not be an unacceptable risk and, after all, he was being asked actually to re-write a story he had already written. When the research is being done properly, before the story is composed, the search for colourful detail and convincing background can make reading extremely purposeful and thereby very absorbing and useful.

Choosing Books for Topic Work

The type of book-based tasks that we have been discussing so far suggests two important questions for teachers to ask when they come to select books either for use in a particular topic, or for the class library. First, is the book coherent? Does it lend itself to the setting of note-making, summarising tasks, which involve either the whole book or fairly long sections of it? Are there worthwhile concepts which a child can pursue through reasonably long sections of the book, as the question of changing use of building materials could be followed through *Building*?

It is usually fairly obvious whether a given book is going to lend itself to the 'note-making' approach, but applying the second test on the usefulness of small sections of the book for the setting of intensive batches of questions and tasks takes a bit longer. Suppose, for instance, a section of text reads like this:

> This is a car. (picture) It has an engine to drive it, and the engine uses fuel called petrol. Here is another way of travelling. It is a train. (picture) It also has an engine to drive it, and it uses diesel fuel.

This text suggests worthwhile questions like 'What other things driven by engines do we travel in? Do you know what sort of fuel they use? What would happen if we ran out of fuel? What sorts of things could we travel in that don't use fuel?' There is an obvious, important set of things to think about here, and the text leads the way into thinking about those things. If, however, the text were to go on:

> Aircraft, ships, helicopters, motor-bikes, motor-boats, all use fuel to drive their engines. If the world ran out of fuel, they would all have to stop. Perhaps people would have to use sailing ships again, or horses, or just walk everywhere

then these questions would have been closed out, and we would have to cast around for others. Very often, a superficially attractive and interesting text makes itself less useful than it could be, by doing children's thinking for them, and leaving simply no room for reflection or speculation by the child. At the other extreme, a text can be excessively bland. If our text read simply 'This is a car. (picture) This is a train. (picture) Many people can travel in the train', then we would have to cast about for our own problem or unifying concept — such as fuel-use, to act as a focus for questioning, which would multiply our difficulties. A question like 'What do cars and trains have in common?' does not necessarily yield the answer 'They both need fuel'. 'Why can many people travel in the train?', the only question suggested directly by the text, is a silly question. This text is not necessarily unusable, but, it is unhelpful. To check whether the general style of the book is to be unhelpfully bland, excessively 'helpful' so as to close out promising lines of questioning, or to hit the happy medium which raises questions without answering them, we need to check half-a-dozen pages or sections and actually try setting a group of tasks or questions using a reasonable range of skills. If we can't make it work one time in two, then the book is not going to suit our particular style of questioning.

A second criterion in book selection is the skill with which the author introduces new concepts, or concepts that might be new, to the reader. The rate of introduction is one important factor:

> The lesser nobles or gentry called 'Samurai' were the chief warriors of Japan, and their adventures and battles were made into legends and myths, in later times.

'noble', 'lesser nobles', 'gentry', 'Samurai', 'legends' and 'myths' are all introduced (for the first time in the book) in 27 words. They are all concepts of some difficulty, but are introduced with such speed and so close together as to make one assume that the intended audience must already have a pretty good grasp of them. Yet the book's format — large print and numerous pictures — all suggest a junior school readership.

The second key factor in the introduction of new concepts is well illustrated by these two pages (both actually written by older children for younger children):

> On the great plains the Indians led a wandering life. They followed the buffalo from place to place, living in tents and carrying all they owned on horses. They were what we called NOMADS.

Nomad Indians wandered the great plains of America. They hunted the buffalo and were great fighters.

Obviously the first passage at least tries to prepare the way for the new concept 'nomad', by talking about wanderings, tents and portable possessions. In the second passage, 'Nomad' could legitimately be taken to mean 'red', 'fierce', 'friendly', or almost anything else — it could even be the name of a tribe, and not much in the text that follows clarifies the matter.

Readability

With young learners, of course, we have the problem that as well as not grasping a newly introduced concept, they may actually not be. able to read the unfamiliar word in which it is embodied. This brings us to the question of the 'readability' of a book, in its technical sense, which also must clearly be a vital criterion in book-selection. Matching the readability of text to the reading-skill of the children is a major part of the teacher's role in any area, and there is a range of literature which goes very fully into this question, such as *An Investigation into Alternative Methods of Assessing the Readability of Books used in School* (Heallie, S. & Ramsey, E., Ward Lock, 1971) and 'A Formula for Predicting Readability' (Dale, E. & Chall, J.S., *Educational Research Bulletin*, vol. 27, 1948). Factors like the legibility of the print, the size of the print, the length of sentences and of paragraphs operate across the board of children's reading material, and it is not the brief of this book to go into the general subject of readability as such. One aspect of 'readability' in general, though, has strong echoes in the particular matter of choosing books for topic work and that is precisely the question of 'predictability' alluded to in the discussion of the two passages above on 'nomads'.

As the meaning of a new word is easier to grasp if we are given clues about that meaning before we meet the word, so a word is actually easier to read if its placing in the sentence, and the surrounding words, give us clues as to what kind of word it might be. A good example would be a foreign word like 'Sioux', which is always going to be difficult to read because of its bizarre, 'un-English' spelling. If we present it like this, though — 'One of the Indian tribes was called Sioux', the reader, before meeting the word at all, knows to expect a proper name, may already know the sound of that particular name from television and, at worst, is not too surprised or disheartened if it turns out to be a funny word and he has to ask the teacher what it is. If we had written it like this, though — 'The Sioux were one of the Indian tribes', then the young reader is grappling straight away with the word helped only by the very slender clue provided by 'the'. In this situation, children have read 'Sioux' as 'six', 'suit', 'shaky', 'slow', or been reduced to the sheer desperation of 'people', and 'bison', all of them reasonable candidates to follow the word 'the'. If our author has the skill to introduce both new concepts, and words which are intrinsically hard to read, with a proper regard for this need for contextual clues then this will be a very important 'plus' on the side of choosing the book.

Books, of course, are rarely chosen by teachers, or liked or disliked by children, on the strength of their text alone. Pictures in books these days are frequently excellent and exciting in themselves, fruitful sources of questions and tasks, and sometimes very intimately related to understanding and using the text. They can even constitute a good reason for using the book when the text is quite unsatisfactory. However, readers may find it a useful exercise at this point to consider the books represented by the following extracts purely on the basis of their texts, assuming (correctly) that each book has good pictures, but deciding on the basis of the extracts alone whether or not the book would be useful for work with their own particular classes, in connection with a topic on 'work'.

Exercise 2

Extract A (*What Happens When — You Throw Things Away* by Gerard Bell, Oliver & Boyd, 1975)

MORE AND MORE RUBBISH! WHERE CAN I PUT IT ALL?
Mrs. Shaw has a problem. She always seems to have more rubbish than her dustbin will hold. Her husband is the Cleansing Officer for a city of half a million people. So Mr. Shaw has the same problem as his wife — but multiplied half a million times.

The Shaw family throw many different kinds of refuse (another name for rubbish) into their bin: paper, metal, wood, plastic and glass, as well as ashes, dust and scraps of food. Can you think of other kinds of refuse that go into a family dustbin?

Mrs. Shaw rinses out food tins and wraps food scraps in paper parcels before putting them in her bin. If she did not, the food would smell and attract flies — and flies carry disease.

She keeps clean paper in a separate box for the refuse men to take away. Do you know why she does this?

Extract B (*What Happens When — You Throw Things Away*)
This is the dust-cart which takes away the Shaws' rubbish once a week. As the men empty the bins into the cart, a special machine inside compresses the rubbish — that is, presses it down very tightly. The cart can hold 50 cubic metres of refuse. Can you work out roughly how many years the Shaw family would take to fill the cart?

Ordinary dustbins would be no use for a factory which has a lot of rubbish to get rid of. The refuse is put into a large box called a container. Every few days, a lorry brings a fresh, empty container and takes the full one away to be emptied. Containers can be cleaned out and used again.

Extract C (*Daddy Drives a Bus* by Anita Harper, Blackie)
Jill knows that different people do different jobs when they go to work. Jill's daddy's job is driving a bus.

Now Jill has noticed quite a lot about buses. She knows that some are double deckers and some are single deckers. Most of the ones she sees are red, but sometimes, when she goes to other towns she sees buses that are green or yellow or blue.

One day Jill asks if she can see her daddy driving his bus. 'Yes' says her mother, 'if we get up early tomorrow we can go to work with daddy'.

Extract D (*Daddy Drives a Bus*)
The bus went back along the same roads but everything looked a bit different because they were going the other way. They stopped at the bus stops on the other side of the road this time and Ted rang the bell, ting, ting, when the people had finished getting off, just like he did before.

'I wonder where all these people are going?' said Jill.

'I think some of them are going to work and some are going to the shops and some are boys and girls going to school' said her mother.

Sometimes they saw other buses with different numbers on and they were going to different places. Soon they got back to the bus garage and the bus was empty again.

Extract E (*The Reporter* by Michael Pollard, Macmillan)
What's the news? We all want to know.

The reporter's job is to tell us. All over the world, reporters are working to let us know what's going on.

In a city in Asia there is fighting in the streets. A reporter is there to tell us what it's like.

A statesman visits London from abroad. Reporters write down what he says and does.

A train crashes. A reporter is sent to describe the scene.

A famous sportsman is being married. Reporters and photographers are there to record the event.

Extract F (The Reporter)

The Newsroom

When he is not out on a story, the reporter works in a *newsroom*. The *news editor* decides which stories are to go into the paper.

When someone invites the paper to send a reporter to something that's happening the news editor writes the details down in a big diary and chooses one of his reporters to go.

Often, when he is out on a job, a reporter has to write very quickly. He might be listening to a speech, or making a list of names and addresses. If he wrote his notes out in ordinary writing, he could never keep up. So most reporters learn *shorthand*, a quick form of writing. Later, when they get back to the newsroom, they turn their shorthand back into ordinary writing or typing.

Notes on Exercises

Exercise 1 – Comments and Suggestions

Anything we say about these extracts as learning materials is bound to be somewhat unfair, as in each case the text is accompanied and often illuminated by pictures, and in many cases questions on the pictures could supplement or even replace questions on the text. That having been said, we will approach the text as text:

Extract A is a very useful one from our point of view – why men 'did not build houses', why, having settled in caves they ever left them, why some people built in wood and others in stone, are all questions raised by this passage, and they are all questions connected with fundamental concepts about man's relationship with his environment.

Extract B raises questions about the morality of inflicting pain, about the social fact that it is commonly girls, not boys who undergo processes of 'beautification' and about changes in tastes and fashions.

What do people do to themselves today to look nice? Is it girls who do things more than boys? Why? — all these commend themselves as questions.

Extract C 'Off-the-peg' as a phrase might be a good candidate for explanation in the child's own words, but the important idea underlying this extract is an economic one, that made-to-measure clothes cost more, and that some people are willing to pay that extra cost. The first thing to establish would be the fact of the greater cost, and then the reasons for it, if the child can grasp the associated idea of intensity of labour.

Extract D The phrases 'relay team' (emphasised in the original) could be explained by the child, but the most important and penetrating question here is 'What was in these messages that men had to risk their lives to carry them?' The question is certainly not closed off by the text, in fact it is arguably left excessively open, with no clue of any kind offered. It would be very interesting to see what kind of answers your children would give to such a question.

Extract E This is an interesting passage in itself, but it is unfortunate that the last dozen words close out the young reader from speculating about the advantages of the special railway, making exploitation of the passage by the teacher difficult.

6 CHILDREN'S DAY-TO-DAY EXPERIENCES

What we have tried to emphasise in this book is the need for teachers to use the vast amount of information available to them and to the children they teach as a means of achieving much more worthwhile learning than the information itself provides for. By this we mean that we cannot expect a child to retain more than a mere fraction of the information which he is likely to acquire. In any event, the learning of information poses an impossible problem of selection since, apart from the incredible store of factual information already available, each day will add further to that store as new events occur, new discoveries are made and so on.

In addition, the demands made on the child by the teacher whose main concern is for the child to acquire his own stock of factual information are very limited indeed. The child can be required to recall the information he has learned and to record it in a variety of ways. This may provide for useful practice in writing or such but provides little in the way of understanding. Indeed a child can be very successful in learning recalling and recording information without any understanding of it at all. What is equally unfortunate is that the teacher whose expectations of his pupils are at the level of information retention and recall can appear to be a very successful teacher with pupils able to answer correctly a host of questions.

For example, we could require children to learn that Tegucigalpa is the capital of Honduras and the diligent child will be able to answer such questions as

'What is the capital of Honduras?'
'Where is Tegucigalpa?'
'What is Tegucigalpa?'

The difficulty is when the child is asked to explain the information in some way. 'What is meant by a capital?' or 'List some reasons why Tegucigalpa might be the capital of Honduras?' Questions like that require the child to have an understanding of what a capital city is — what are its characteristics. The quality of his answers will depend on the extent to which his idea or concept of a capital is developed.

So our concern in this book is to encourage teachers to help their pupils to process information in ways that will help them to develop both a range of intellectual skills or thinking strategies, and a complex of developing conceptual understanding, around which the children can organise new experiences and begin to understand them. Having such understanding helps when a new situation presents itself since few experiences are absolutely unique. There is always likely to be aspects of the new experience which whilst not exactly replicating past experiences will have similarities. The fact that Tegucigalpa is the capital of Honduras may be a completely new piece of information but if they have processed the idea of a capital in other contexts, e.g. London, and at an appropriate level as a place which is the centre of commerce, government, culture, etc., then the new piece of information is not at all problematic – the child has a 'pigeonhole' in which to slot it. If children are to understand their world and to organise the mass of information coming in then they need such a sorting arrangement, a developing set of ideas or concepts. Such concepts will only be formed if the thinking experiences the child undergoes and the occasions on which he is required to enumerate items, group them according to given criteria, give explanations of and make judgements about them and so on, are numerous and structured. In this way teachers will be providing for children to transfer their understanding in one situation (about London as a capital) to another situation (about Tegucigalpa) and in this way not only facilitating further learning but also the expectation that whatever is learned will be worthwhile in that it will be used in new and different ways in the future. This critical matter of conceptual understanding and transfer of understanding is dealt with in greater detail in Part One.

Nevertheless, no such development can take place unless the teacher provides and/or uses sources of information which are likely to provide for useful ideas to be developed.

One of the most prolific sources of such information lies within the child's own day-to-day experience. Every day the child is involved in a vast range of experiences at first hand. In addition, through the medium of television he is likely to be provided with a huge range of vicarious experiences. Whilst some of the material and information available to children through watching television may not be what we would choose ourselves, there will be a lot which will add usefully to a child's stock of information and with which teachers might work. Both sources will provide the child with experience of his own or of others' contacts with family members, with friends, with teachers, shop keepers, bus conductors, policemen, lollipop ladies and so on. Most children are aware of and have some actual contact with institutions and events in the community. They will have been in the supermarket, perhaps in the bank, the church, the library, the town hall, the fire station. They will have heard and seen something of elections and voting, of people at work, the policeman, the fireman, the school nurse and the factory worker or farmer.

These contacts and experiences can be used very effectively by the teacher to provide the child with a developing insight into a great range of ideas, since they provide very 'concrete' pegs on which to hang important concepts and understandings.

For example, the young child lives in a family and will know from the first-hand experience the importance of relations between people, although he may not formally understand much at this stage about family 'roles' or their relationship to social organisation. A closer look at typical family incidents may however improve the child's understanding, give him some understanding of the way people behave towards him.

Such incidents will include such problem-type situations as deciding which TV programme to watch; deciding whether or not to have a pet and talking about the responsibilities involved; the problem of moving house and going to live in the country instead of the city; or to a high rise flat without a garden. Some families have to cope with problems such as parents working on shifts or permanently at night or away from home a lot. Children experience additions to their family group — a new brother or sister; of mother going into hospital perhaps; or going out to work. The family is affected too by such matters as the child moving from infant to junior school. All such experiences are a source of information the teacher ought not to ignore.

It may be argued that many of these experiences within the family, and those detailed later on in this chapter, will not be particularly interesting or provide the kind of motivating, exciting approach to topic work many teachers like to develop. This need not be so, since many of the ideas suggested in this chapter can be incorporated in imaginary situations such as that involving a group of people shipwrecked on a desert island that is developed in some detail on pages 167-81. In other cases, topics which the teacher already knows are successful in terms of motivation can have included within them opportunities for the child to consider situations, involving people, which are similar to the ones he will have experienced himself.

A topic on 'pets' might, for instance, include some situation where a child — Tony — wants to have a big dog as a pet but Tony's mother is against the idea.

> Why should she take that line?
> How might the disagreement be resolved?

It may be that the children will suggest different ways of resolving the problem:

(a) by compromise. Tony gets a small dog not the big Alsatian he wanted; or

(b) by agreement. Tony agrees to train and look after the dog, clear up any mess it makes, contribute to its cost out of pocket money and so on. To put it in a high-sounding way, Tony takes on duties and obligations in return for a privilege (having a dog).

So we have used our topic on pets to get quite naturally into important social studies ideas with the children — duties, compromise, the possibility of settling conflicts by agreement — and indeed have begun to develop ideas about the way in which groups operate, how they demand responsibility and some self-sacrifice from their members. He begins to see the value of co-operating in decision making and is on the way to understanding higher level political concepts such as democracy, which are built on lower level ideas such as 'agreement', 'compromise' and 'duties'. Choosing which concepts to develop is not easy, and elsewhere in this book this matter of concept selection is dealt with in some detail, but those ideas we have mentioned above are self-evidently important in helping a child to understand how different groups are organised and how they operate, using the family as the basic group of which most children will have experienced membership.

Exercise 1

Think up some simple family situation which most children may have experienced where there is an element of disagreement. Describe the situation to the children so as to introduce them to a further example of the matter of decision making and related ideas.

Get the children to suggest how the disagreement might best be resolved. Allow them to act out the situation in groups, draw 'strip' cartoon-type pictures and write down their ideas.

Allow for a discussion of the various ideas that will be put forward so as to reinforce the idea that there are a number of ways by which agreement might be reached.

Another important set of concepts which might be introduced through a wide variety of topics is that of 'authority', 'rules' and 'law'. All groups have rules for their members and some system of establishing and exercising authority. The child who belongs to several groups will have first-hand experience of having to recognise and obey authority; having to learn and obey rules and perhaps of disobeying rules; coming into conflict with authority and suffering the consequences. The more impersonal idea of law is simply an extension of the understanding the child needs to develop about authority and the reasons why groups need rules and how they not only keep order within the group but serve to protect group members.

The idea of authority can be introduced in a wide variety of topics and especially those where people wearing uniforms are part of the context. Uniforms are worn for a variety of reasons which the children can be asked to reason about — protection, identity, membership, etc., but also authority. However, children will be aware through their own experience that different people have different levels of authority and this can be used to develop understanding about such matters as the limitations of authority and the reasons for this. For example, a police-man can arrest you but does not send you to prison, a bus conductor can turn you off the bus if you misbehave but does not arrest you, the lollipop lady can stop you crossing the road but cannot send you to bed, a teacher tells you what to do at school but parents tell you what to do at home. Sorting out the reasons will involve asking why we need the lollipop lady, the policeman, the soldier, etc., and why there are different degrees of authority — the sergeant in the police force, the headteacher at school and officers in the army. A major intention of this work with the children will be to develop their understanding of the idea that authority is bestowed upon an individual by the community, which itself also makes up the rules of the community and whose permission we often have to have to do certain things — for example, drive a car, alter our house in certain ways or own a television set. Getting children to think about such things as these will provide for the development of worthwhile knowledge about the nature of society at neighbourhood level, the kind of alternatives that are open to society and how the rules and decisions made by a community are representative of that community's values.

There are a number of other aspects about understanding the way in which rules operate which seem important. One is that the different groups the child belongs to — family, school, games teams, scouts and guides — will have slightly different sets of rules. A second is that rules may differ according to the age of the person, the going-to-bed rule for a twelve year old is likely to be different to that for an eight year old. The aim of the teacher must be to help children to see the reasons for rules and the reasons for differences between groups, and individuals within groups, in relation to the rules that are applied. It may also be useful to devise activities that will help children see that there will be differences between groups — especially family groups — which are there by virtue of different values. There should indeed be no attempt to form a set of family rules. If one child is allowed to watch television whilst eating his tea and another child is not, the thing to be teased out is not that one rule is right and the other wrong, but that there is a difference between the two families and each has a reason for making the rule.

Whatever the topic in which the idea of rules is to be introduced, it might be useful first to establish the idea of different group membership and the fact that different rules apply to each group.

This might be done by writing on the board or on a series of cards a mixed list of rules such as:

Walk quietly down the corridor.
No right turn.
No television until after tea.
If you hit the ball straight to a player on the fielding side who catches it before it touches the ground you are out.
Do not cross the road until the green man appears.
Knock and wait.
Keep off the grass.
Brush your teeth before going to bed.
Line up by the gate and wait for the teacher to tell you to get on the bus.
Do not touch the saucepans on the cooker.

The children can be asked to suggest where they might be or which group they would be acting as a member of when they were obeying each rule. They could be asked to put the rules into separate lists with an appropriate heading for each, such as:

At home.   In school.   Cricket team.   In the street.

They could be asked to think up additional rules to add to each list and perhaps to write a list of rules for some other group they belong to.

The next step will be to get the children to discuss the reasons for the rules — if you can run about and shout on the school field, why do you have to walk quietly in the corridor? It may be useful to get the children to consider a situation such as the following and to write, draw or act out what they feel will be the consequences and perhaps to devise a rule that will ensure the situation does not arise again.

> Trevor and Mary are playing tag in the garden and with all that running about they get very hot and thirsty. They go into the kitchen to get a drink of orange juice but the bottle is empty. Trevor opens the fridge and takes out a bottle of milk which he and Mary have a good drink from so that there is only a little bit left in the bottom when they have finished. They put the bottle back in the fridge and are just on their way out again when Mum rushes in saying she has almost forgotten to make the custard for Dad's evening meal.

Exercise 2

Make up a similar situation in story form so that the children can act out, draw or write about the way other people are affected when someone breaks a rule.

Exercise 3

Think up two or three class rules designed to make the classroom a pleasant place where everyone can get on with the job of learning (or teaching). Discuss your reasons for making these rules with the children and take a vote on whether they should be adopted.

Get the children to think up additional rules and by a process of discussion and voting, choose the five or six everyone thinks are essential.

Print the list and post it up in the classroom.

Exercise 4

Make up a list of preliminary questions you might ask when preparing the children before they write a story which begins: 'When, I am . . . I shall be able to . . .'

So far we have considered in this chapter how a child's day-to-day experience can be the basis from which he can be taught two important understandings about the society that he lives in, i.e. that society is made up of groups which exist to take care of their members and that all groups have rules which they expect their members to obey. In several of the exercises the method suggested for providing the children with appropriate information is to tell them a story. Most teachers will be adept at making up such short stories and will be aware of their value in motivating children towards paying attention, in developing a sense of empathy with the characters involved and in general participating in the activities to which the story leads. Remember however that the stories suggested here have a definite learning function – the development of conceptual understanding and intellectual skills. They will provide for this best if they are:

(a) reasonably short;
(b) are about named persons the children can identify with;
(c) are about problems which are of the kind the children can recognise as being likely in the context of the story plot;
(d) are written so as to include plenty of dialogue between the various characters;
(e) give rise to a variety of questions which will help the children to consider the problems raised in as many different ways as possible.

For example in the topic on 'pets' an aspect that might be included as we have already suggested is the problem of deciding whether to have a pet at all, or which kind of pet to have. Considering these problems will introduce children to such important ideas as co-operation and compromise, social responsibility, rules and law and economics.

The problems associated with choosing and keeping a pet might well be introduced by a story which begins:

PETS

Stephen is hurrying home from school. 'If only Mum says "Yes" ' he is thinking. Stephen's best friend Paul has a baby rabbit for anyone who is willing to give it a home. Stephen would love to have a rabbit for a pet. As soon as he opens the door and sees his mother Stephen tells her of his plan. There is a box in the shed at the bottom of the garden where the rabbit can live. He has even thought of a name for it and he can fetch it after tea.

His mother tells him to stop a minute. 'We can't choose a pet in two seconds', she says, 'We'll talk about it when your Dad comes home – though I don't think he will want a rabbit.'

Mum is right. Stephen's Dad does not like the idea of keeping a rabbit but he has always wanted a dog. He says, 'Now the children are older Mary, they will be able to look after a dog properly.' Dad pointed out that all you can do with rabbits is feed them and clean them out. You can't take a rabbit for a run and a game of ball like you can with a puppy.

"Can we have a Collie, then, like Lassie?' asks Stephen. But Dad thinks they will have to get a dog that will not cost so much and will be easier to look after. 'What about a Fox Terrier', he says. "I'd rather have a quieter dog' declares Mum. 'Why don't we have a Saluki then? A lot of pop singers have Salukis', says Stephen's elder sister Sue.

The family cannot decide but plan to go and look for a puppy the very next Saturday. Stephen can think of nothing else. Dad suggests to him that he ought to try and find out as much as possible about looking after a dog properly before Saturday comes. 'All right Dad', says Stephen, 'but I know where there is a good place to get a puppy from. Joe's Pet Stall on the market. He always has lovely puppies.' 'Don't you think the Pet Shop in the High Street would be better', says Sue. 'Or perhaps it might be worth driving out to the kennels at Oakton. Yes, what's what we will do', decides Dad.

After the children have gone to bed Dad began to think about all the things they would have to do before the puppy arrived. For instance he would have to look at the garden tomorrow. 'Jim Smith next door is very proud of his garden and there is the busy road too', thinks Dad, 'I must talk to the children about the things they will have to do. Puppies need taking out for a walk quite often and as they get older need a lot of exercise.'

'What a good job the Council didn't put us in the flats', says Mum looking at the lights blazing from the high block as she draws the curtains. 'They don't allow pets there you know!'

At last Saturday is here. A very excited family set out for the kennels. Stephen jumps out of the car first. It takes quite a long time to look at all the different puppies that are for sale. Some are sleepy, some are yapping, some are chasing their brothers and sisters but the one that they all like the best is a lively little Jack Russell terrier. He comes straight to Stephen and licks his hand, just as though he is choosing the family and not the other way round. 'Let's have this one', begs Stephen. Everyone agrees he really is a lovely puppy. The kennel owner tells Dad how easy Jack Russells are to train and so it is decided and Dad gets his cheque book out.

'The vet is here every Friday so you can bring him back for his injections', says the kennel owner. He also tells them not to begin obedience training too soon. 'Not until he is about five months old. In the meantime be patient with him and give him a lot of affection', he says.

'Let's call him Chum', says Stephen.

When they get home Stephen shows Chum around his new home. He plays with him and gives him some puppy food in his new bowl. When it is bedtime Mum wraps a warm hot water bottle in an old blanket. The puppy snuggles up to it, tired after a busy day and is soon fast asleep.

Chum likes his new home and his new family and the family like their new pet. They have a lot of good times together and all is going well until . . . One morning Mum opens the front door to get in the milk and Chum, who is looking for an adventure slips out and into the road before anyone notices. He thinks how clever he is to be walking alone down the pathway and he begins to explore. He turns this way and that but when he decides to go home he cannot find the way. He is lost.

Meanwhile at home everyone is very worried. Where can Chum be? Stephen looks in every road on the estate. He goes down all the paths he usually takes Chum on his walks but there is no sign of him. When Dad comes home Chum is still missing.

'We should tell the police', says Dad.

Later a very worried Stephen goes with his Dad to the police station. The officer asks a lot of questions and says that if they hear anything he will let them know. When Stephen goes to bed that night he is very sad indeed.

Exercise 5

Enlarge the outline story about Trevor and Mary and the custard on page 88. Decide which particular aspects of the idea of 'rules' you wish to develop.

Another important understanding about society which is accessible by way of childrens' own experience, is that society is changing all the time. This idea of social change is an important one for children to understand. They have also to come to realise that things do not just change, but that there are quite specific reasons for changes taking place — changes in values for example or advances in technology. They need too to come to understand that change affects different people in different ways. This understanding, as it develops, will help the child to cope with change in his own life both now and in the future which is an essential ability in our constantly changing world.

There is plenty of evidence of change in the home. There will be new equipment bought for the house, double glazing put in, perhaps, or the child moves from one house to another with better conditions and facilities. In addition there will be visits to the houses of relatives and visits to building sites and the show houses on them or to demolition sites or museums which have replicas of rooms in earlier houses.

From all these sources will come evidence of change — changes that have taken place because new ideas and new machines have made it possible for houses to be warmer, easier to manage and so on and because people have developed different values and want a different kind of life than their parents and grandparents had.

So in a topic on 'my family' or on 'houses' or 'homes' the teacher might pose the question — 'How and why is the house you live in different from the house your grandma lived in when she was a little girl?'

If we answered this question for ourselves we might come up with such suggestions as:

Grandma's house would be difficult to keep warm in winter as it had coal fires. Many modern houses have central heating.
Coal fires create a lot of work, are dirty and go out at night. Central heating is clean and automatic.
Vacuum cleaners, running hot water and washing machines make the running of a modern home much easier. Grandma would do the cleaning and washing by hand.

This sort of information ought to provide for quite a lot of work over several topic sessions. Such work, in addition to developing the children's understanding that changes do take place, will introduce or reintroduce the children to ideas such as values, technological advance, efficiency, labour-saving and other new vocabulary. As they process this information the children will practise and develop a range of intellectual skills such as translation, interpretation, evaluation and extrapolation. They will learn too to exercise empathy with people who are affected by change.

How can the teacher achieve such objectives using this information about change? What can the children do? They could talk to Grandma and Grandad asking them to describe the house they lived in as children. They can make lists (by themselves or with the teacher) of similarities and differences (classification) between then and now. The teacher could make or draw pretend dustbins with items to simulate rubbish thrown away then and now. In Great Grandma's dustbin, ashes, greaseproof paper, vegetable peelings. In Mum's dustbin, tin, packets, etc. Children to discuss or write about differences and explain them (interpretation and inference). They could draw pictures of Mum's day and Great Grandma's day.

e.g.	Great Grandma	Mum
6.00 a.m.	Lighting fires	Asleep — central heating comes on
7.00 a.m.	Getting hot water boiler going to do washing	Asleep — house nice and warm

etc.

They could write or tell the teacher who they would prefer to be and why. (Evaluation.) They could ask Grandma/Grandad what they don't like about the changes (empathy) and why, and talk about them or write about them. e.g. too much television and no conversation, or no coal fires. They could act out a scene in the Wendy House to show differences in:

— amount of work

— kind of work

— amount of time for leisure

They could help the teacher make a class frieze. This could, for example, show such things as:

a) how long it took Great Grandma to:

i) clean the house

ii) make the dinner etc.

b) Great Grandma's house in winter

— no insulation

— no central heating

— no electric light, draughts, etc.

Our house

— insulated

— double glazed

— warm and bright etc.

The older children could write a little story as if they were their Grandma when she was young — what was good, what was not so good. (translation/empathy).

They could write about, talk about, draw what it would be like if:

— there were no vacuum cleaners

— no central heating

— no tinned food etc.

— no refrigerators (extrapolation)

They could talk to Mum and try to list the things she would miss most if she didn't have them and classify them in some way.

e.g.   those that save a lot of time, e.g. instant foods

those that save a lot of hard work, e.g. washing machines.

Getting to understand the cause and effects of change in this context will help the children later on to understand about it in other contexts.

Exercise 6

Change occurs in every aspect of life and ever social group and institution. Almost any social studies-based topic therefore could deal with change as one of its themes. Children are aware of a great many things about shops, for example, both from their own experience of shopping locally and in the larger towns or cities and from what they see on television or in films and books or have recounted to them by older relatives. Devise a series of tasks for children who are considering the changes that have taken place over recent years in relation to shops and shopping and the causes and effects of those changes.

Teachers ought too to make use of the information the child will already have about an important aspect of social behaviour — work. Whilst the school may need to add considerably to the child's stock of information about work there is no doubt, as was mentioned earlier in this chapter, that many of the contacts and observations within the child's day-to-day experience will be concerned with people working. They will see men working on building sites, delivering goods to shops and repairing telephone lines or electric cables. They will see people in the school stoking the central heating plant and preparing the school meal. They will visit the clinic and be attended to by doctors and nurses, they may visit banks, laundrettes and petrol stations with their parents. They will probably have travelled on one-man buses, seen the meter reader doing his job or answered the door to the rent collector. Certainly they will all have some knowledge of the postman, the milkman, have been in shops and, of course, seen teachers at work.

This vast store of information available to the teacher can be used to develop a wide range of understandings about such matters as work, responsibility, efficiency, technology, authority, supply and demand, interdependence, job satisfaction and so on. Such ideas can be developed if the child is required to manipulate the information as he answers such questions as:

— What is X doing?
— Have you seen Mr Smith doing his work?
— Why is he doing it?
— How does the machinery help him?
— How does the work he does help other people?
— Who is the most important person in the shop — or school — or building site?
— What will he do next?
— Is the job difficult?
— Which job takes longer to learn?

These ideas are developed more fully in the topic on 'People and Work' which is considered in detail in Appendix II.

7 'INDIRECT APPROACHES'

This chapter deals with three types of children's activity — drawing and painting; outside visits, drama and 'discussion'. All three have in common that they can make very valuable contributions to children's education and specifically to their progress in the social studies 'topic' area. They have another thing in common — their worthwhileness in a particular situation, and the usefulness of their outcomes in a particular situation, are much more difficult to evaluate than is the case with more straightforward activities, such as questions based on pictures or books.

This difficulty about evaluating these more 'indirect approaches' to learning has led people sometimes to conclude that they are in fact impossible to evaluate at all, and then, by a logical leap, to decide that as activities they are self-evidently good things in themselves, not subject to the normal rude questions like 'What's the point of all this?' 'What did the children learn?' which come the way of straightforward writing or mathematical tasks. This complacency is of course reinforced by children's legitimate enthusiasm for the activities. Everybody likes going on visits and acting in plays, and drawing is such a popular and easily organised activity that it is quite commonly used as a device to get people to do less popular forms of work — 'Finish six questions and then you can draw'.

Drawing and Painting

So what kind of goals can teachers have for these activities, and how can success be evaluated? If we start with painting/drawing we see straightaway that there is a philosophical difficulty. If we set someone to draw and paint a shop front we might look for the following things from, as it were, the 'social studies' point of view:

(1) a door and large window;
(2) some kind of name, prominently displayed, either of a type of shop or the shop's owner or 'co-op' or whatever;
(3) some goods in the window appropriate to the type of shop in question.

These three features would be the minimum we would expect to see from a child showing that they understood the fundamental idea of a shop. We would be very pleased to see evidence of further understandings and social observation such as a 'Special Offer' sign, appropriate people near the shop (such as children looking at a toyshop window), a delivery van outside, in short, anything that showed understanding of the nature and purposes of shops.

However, it is quite possible that all these features are present, but that the picture is badly executed in some way — the paint, for instance, may have been applied so unskilfully as to make John dissatisfied with the result viewed as a painting. In other words, 'success' from the social studies viewpoint might be aesthetic failure or, of course, the other way round. On the face of it, we can quite happily use two sets of criteria: we can note that John knows a lot about shops but is not very good at painting. The difficulty of simultaneously operating in both 'art' and 'social studies' arises when we think about what we are going to get John to do next. It may be that it was precisely his praiseworthy ambition on the 'social studies' side which led him to depict a supermarket, with delivery vans, wire trolleys, dozens of different types of goods, etc., when his skills with paint were of such a level that the subject was overambitious.

If our next drawing/painting task is a factory, do we advise John to keep it simple, and not try to show fork-lift trucks, bus-loads of workers, delivery lorries and all the other things he knows are associated with factories, but may have trouble painting? Or do we encourage him to go on beyond his present limits of skill with paint and producing things which please us, but may be seen by him as fiascos, and which may discourage his aesthetic development?

There is no final answer to this dilemma, but the best expedient is to try to set up expectations about drawing and painting connected directly with the topic which stress that this is one way of expressing understanding and conveying information about important questions and that it is the information and understanding which matters. Quite often, there will be no conflict anyway, and we can praise both the 'Special Offer' sign and the striking colours in which it is painted, but in the case of John, we could encourage him to use stick-figures if he cannot draw people to his own satisfaction; to depict a delivery van if necessary as a mere oblong with 'delivery van' written on it; to use paint only on those parts of the picture where it is helpful, such as the shop-name, and so on. We can then look to his aesthetic development in tasks where the goals are unequivocally aesthetic, and where everybody knows what is expected of them quite clearly.

One of the criteria by which to evaluate 'topic' drawing as such has been made clear in the example on 'shops'; that is, basically, comprehensiveness when children are called upon to illustrate some concept such as 'shop', 'factory', 'harbour', 'castle', 'farm', 'zoo', 'school', which lends itself to static representation.

If the set of ideas to be represented is very complicated, then a series of pictures, perhaps linked up as a frieze, is the technique to use. Depicting 'life in a village in India' for instance might involve showing hard agricultural work, simple housing, primitive machinery, an outdoor village school, irrigation and other features, which it would take the skill of a Breughel to put into one picture. If, however, the problem is divided up, and a frieze is the result, we must be careful that each segment of the frieze sets a worthwhile problem for the child doing that segment. It would not be too difficult to show people working, but the child must be set the problem of showing, somehow, that they are working *hard*, and that their tools are primitive. If a given task of this kind is too difficult, then the child must be encouraged to use captions and labels — to show, for instance, that the Indian children at the outdoor school only have one or two hours schooling a day, by means of a picture alone might be possible, but sounds very difficult. Wording a short caption to the picture which makes the point clearly but briefly, would be a much more realistic task. The great danger of frieze work is that ten children get to paint camels, five get to paint palm trees and two children get to paint sand. Every teacher must have observed how it always seems to be the case that these painters of sand, sea, greenery, etc., always seem to be the same children, commonly the least able, or the least assertive. If we avoid this danger, though, collective or frieze-type pictures can enable children as a group to demonstrate pictorially an understanding of quite complex social institutions, such as villages and towns, or industrial and distribution processes.

Friezes are commonly used to depict narrative, especially historical narrative, after the fashion of the Bayeux tapestry. In fact, where we want to depict narrative, and allow children to show their understanding of it, a collectively created frieze is probably not the best way. We could take as an example, a Viking raid. A narrative picture of the raid might show Viking ships appearing; a monk ringing an alarm bell; villagers lighting a beacon, then fleeing; Vikings loading their ships with loot and sailing off; villagers returning to their ruined homes. For a single child to draw individual parts of this story would not be particularly useful — a man, for instance, ringing a bell looks like a man ringing a bell. The problem does not lie, as in the case of an Indian village, in depicting individual meaningful parts of a greater whole, such as the village school or the irrigation system, it lies in depicting the whole narrative, in the right order. A 'strip-cartoon' series of pictures, composed by each individual child will show us whether the characteristics of a raid have been grasped. The good 'strip' will show us attempts to give warnings; the flight of the peaceful inhabitants; the pillaging; the departure of the raiders; and the return of the inhabitants. The presence or absence of these elements, in appropriate order, will give us a good yardstick of evaluation.

Very rough drawings, shading into diagrams or sketch maps can be used as a medium in which children might express their solution to a problem. The two examples (pictures E and F), responses to the problem 'How might the Indian braves catch the wild horses?', show how we can look for both understanding of the specific problem, and advance in the use of conventions, in such sketches.

Picture E

Child E has grasped the importance of approaching the horse-herd downwind, and also has hit on the convenient device of showing the horse-herd merely as a blob as well as conventionalising the cliffs into a zig-zag line. It is not clear what the Indian on top of the cliff is going to do, but the general scheme is clear enough.

Picture F

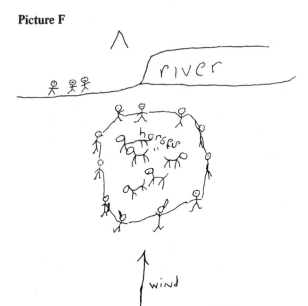

Child F's scheme is much less clear, and his people are approaching upwind. His depiction of 'river' is mysterious, very unclear and neither 'map' nor 'picture'.

The expressing of solutions to problems can go so happily together with progress in mastering the idea of shorthand or conventional representation, in such drawing tasks, that it is surprising that they are not more commonly used.

Visits Outside the School

Any but the briefest of excursions outside the school involves a relatively large investment of time and effort, and therefore the questions 'What's the point?' and 'What did they learn?' are particularly important ones.

The trouble with visits is also their supreme virtue, that is that they are very rich and disordered experiences compared with almost anything that a teacher can organise inside a classroom. The feeling of sitting behind the wheel of a fire-engine, with your feet not quite able to touch a set of huge pedals, looking at a confusing bank of important-looking instruments, can give an inchoate but very strong and immediate insight into what it might mean to be adult, responsible, at work, with frightening power at your fingertips. This understanding could be very valuable, even if we cannot express it clearly in terms of formal learning. At the same time such an experience is likely to be so memorable as to swamp the learnings about 999 calls, firemen's uniforms or whatever, which were the teacher's aims for the visit to the fire-station.

The experiences that visits can give rise to are not just powerful, but as we have just observed 'disordered'. If it were not so, we could expect everybody to be struck by the experience of sitting behind the fire engine wheel and, perhaps, base plans for work on that expectation. However, after a visit to a castle children reported being 'most interested' by the following things:

(1) The rubbish in the well.
(2) What would happen if I fell in the well and could not get out?
(3) Why you have to pay to get in — they have tickets like bus tickets.

Other things had interested other people in the group but these three were not untypical in that they were all quite legitimate preoccupations (1 and 3, at least, could well be the springboard for social-studies learning about the problems of litter and the financing of national monuments); all different, and none of them matched the teacher's concerns and purposes in organising the visit.

None of this necessarily means that we can just regard visits as rich experiences, good things in themselves, standing in no need of further justification. Children are more likely to learn things, in this situation, as in any other, if they know what it is they are supposed to learn, and this need not lead us to using dreary questionnaires about matters of pure fact. Before a fire-station visit, for instance, we could prime children to think about the following questions:

(a) 'Why do you think the station is where it is?' (Interpretation)
(b) 'See who you think is the most important person in the fire-station?' (Evaluation)
(c) 'See if you can find out what would happen if all the fire-engines were out at a fire, and then another fire started?' (Extrapolation)
(d) 'Tell me afterwards what was the most interesting thing you saw or did?' (Evaluation)

The number of questions is small. This is important, as we do not want children to be confused or forever referring to grubby questionnaire sheets. The questions are 'open-ended' and touch on important issues and concepts (such as 'authority' in (b)), and can all be discussed (except (d)) before the visit and any tentative conclusions tested against the reality of the visit. This is also important because it is very easy for a visit to appear to children to be an event disconnected from the rest of the learning process, and this sense of disconnectedness is not much lessened by question-sheets which ask children to count the fire-engines, or perform similar tasks which are plainly more banal and low-level than the work they do in school, and which seem to relate only to the visit, and not to wider issues or ideas. (c) is an important question, as the most sensible way to get an answer is to ask someone at the fire-station, and it is a good idea to introduce children early in their school careers to the idea of a visit as a purposeful inquiry, and to the idea of adults as sources of interesting information which can be elicited by intelligent questions, not just as givers of set lecturettes.

Question (d) leaves the way open for the child to, as it were, legitimise the experiences which seem to him or her to have the most impact, by recording them. The responses may be useable by the teacher, in the context of the general work on the fire-service and public services generally. On the other hand, the 'rich disorder' inherent in the nature of outside visits may manifest itself forcefully, and Terry may be most interested in the station's cat. If he is, we can accept the fact without fuss and without making Terry feel silly — question (d) has already, by its form, legitimised his response — and note again that the very nature of outside visits is such that, in this form of activity more than any other, you can't win them all.

Exercise 1

Devise small groups of three to four questions, in the style of those suggested for the fire-station visit, to use in connection with (i) a visit to a shop or factory, (ii) a visit to an historical site, e.g. a castle.

Children Talking: Discussion

The word 'discussion' is used in many different ways. The following transaction is typical of many in junior schools which are described by teachers and children as 'discussion'.

Teacher: What animals make the best pets, then?

Terry:	Rabbits miss!
Teacher:	Don't call out! – Tell us about rabbits, Terry.
Terry:	You can show them at . . . er . . . I have some and we got a prize.
Lloyd:	Dogs, Alsatians.
Linda:	Budgy.
Teacher:	Yes.
Lloyd:	Snakes.
Many children:	Eeeergh!
Teacher:	Well let's write up a list . . .

Another transaction which could correctly be described as 'discussion' is the following:

Teacher A:	If we take concepts as the main thing in topic work, well, which concepts should we aim at?
Teacher B:	Some people like the idea of a small number of what they call 'key' concepts being useful to hang the whole thing together; make a sort of frame.
Teacher A:	Well, then I think of my topic on 'pets', we got concepts coming up like what counts as a 'pet', 'authority' in the context of who chooses pets, economic ideas about what pet foods cost. I wonder what 'key' concepts could sort of hang that lot together?
Teacher B:	Maybe we could look at one of these lists of 'key' concepts and see if it works out with 'pets' or not.

These transactions are vastly different though both described as 'discussion'. The first is set up and controlled by an authority figure, the teacher; the participants address the teacher, rather than each other; they show no sign of having listened to each other's contributions, they seek rather to get their own contribution in, to 'score' as it were.

The second transaction is 'democratic'. Teacher B seems to know more than Teacher A and has some authority based on that knowledge, but basically this is an exchange between equals. The participants, obviously, address each other, not a third party, and most importantly, they show signs of listening to each other and responding to what the other person says. To put it rather priggishly, they are engaged in a search for truth through discussion, not in a competition to score points.

The gulf between these two sorts of transaction is so great that it is easy to conclude that young children are not capable of 'discussion' in its proper sense at all, but only of taking part in strongly guided question-and-answer sessions. The idea that seems particularly far-fetched is that of children using discussion for its highest purpose, the clarification of issues and the pursuit of truth, and one which implies careful listening to other people, and often the modifying of one's own views in the light of what someone else has said. This idea seems the more far-fetched because a great deal of adult discussion, including, unhappily, most radio and television discussions, is dedicated to scoring points and 'winning', not to clarifying and seeking truth. However, it is worth remembering that some 15 years ago, it would have seemed almost equally implausible that fifteen-year-olds of average to below average abilities could sustain lengthy discussions in a spirit of 'search for truth', referring to evidence, attending to each other's views and modifying their own, especially on emotionally loaded areas like war or poverty. Yet L. Stenhouse and his team, through the Schools Council/Nuffield Humanities Project (Heinemann) showed that with the right techniques and materials, this unlikely goal was in fact quite attainable.

The problem facing the junior teacher in the field of discussion are very different from those facing the teacher of fifteen-year-olds, but Stenhouse's example might encourage us to believe that by taking thought we might find ways to involve children in oral work in which they do more than respond to adult questions, learn to listen to each other and begin to understand the value of discussion as a way of illuminating questions and of learning things.

At some level, children already know about the value of talk. It is not for nothing that very young children keep up a running commentary on what they are doing and what they are going to do: to stop their talk would be to discourage thought. Piaget stresses the importance of discussion bringing about the assimilation and accommodation of new ideas. By this he means more than the acquisition of vocabulary but the incorporation of a new concept into the child's pre-existing conceptual structure, so producing the desired permanent learning. To encourage pupils to use newly acquired concepts in speech, as well as in writing, is important. The problem is how this can be done when a teacher has a large class and limited time. It has been amply demonstrated that teachers are sometimes so pre-occupied with the administration of a class and its activities that their intellectual interaction with children is severely restricted and may occupy an unduly small fraction of time. If this interaction is important, and we would claim it is, then it is urgent that teachers should re-order their priorities and make whatever re-organisation is necessary to allow them to talk with children about the content of topic work. One way of doing so might be to organise activities for say three quarters of the class which require minimum supervision, to allow the teacher to spend 20 minutes in talk with one quarter of the class every day. Does this seem an outrageous demand?

If teachers are to hold such teacher-directed 'discussions' with part of the whole class, they would find it useful to consider some of the techniques initiated by Stenhouse in the context of work with adolescents. Stenhouse urged teachers holding discussions to preserve neutrality, i.e. if asking for his pupils' opinions, they should not reveal by their manner or question what kind of opinion they themselves hold since learners would hesitate to put forward other views. A teacher should similarly not interrupt pupils and should be prepared to wait for them to think about an answer. When a response is received from one child it should not be commented on immediately, in terms of, 'Yes John, that's a good idea', since that is likely to discourage other children from offering varying viewpoints but one should turn to the rest of the group saying 'What does anyone else think?' This all relates to the cultivation of the central ideas, tentativeness and exploratory 'truth-seeking' thinking. As teachers we can all too easily give unmistakable clues as to what we want from a group of children. We can suggest that we are open-minded and genuinely seeking truth or we can indicate equally clearly that children are required to guess our thoughts, and those guessing 'wrong' will be reproved or ignored. Perhaps the best way of all of encouraging exploratory thinking is to show interest in it when it appears; serious and thoughtful consideration of a contribution particularly a tentative one is a much more substantial encouragement than a perfunctory, 'Yes dear, very interesting'.

With older children of eleven or twelve, some innovators have tried organising children into small groups of four or five and setting them some intellectual task. The first time this is tried the task should be both concrete, short and specific, e.g. a history exercise on 'how to capture the castle'. But as the children become accustomed to collaborative work, they can be asked to attempt more exacting tasks, say 'What would happen if the Sahara Desert suddenly had an ample supply of water?' It can be shown that discussions in leaderless groups from which the teacher excludes himself encourage exploratory thinking, the use of new concept words and a wide range of intellectual skills. If such conversations are tape-recorded, however, they may initially appear unimpressive in that children operating at the limits of their understanding may sound incoherent, make false starts, hesitate and do not produce lucid, original, complete sentences. A closer analysis is needed and should be made by reference to the guiding idea of progress in intellectual skills and concepts if the discussion is to be adequately evaluated. When these small group discussions have been concluded, one of the children in each group can be asked to report to the rest what their response to the task is and the teacher can then build on it further.

One matter which ought to form the subject of children's discussion whenever we can arrange it, is the organisation of the children's own work. Earlier in this chapter we referred to the making of a frieze about life in an Indian village, and obviously in the making of such a frieze there are a number of decisions to be taken by somebody, such as the dimensions of the frieze; whether to use paint or some other medium; what order to put the various items in; how to fit in the captions; and so on. Children can usefully discuss these matters, and their decisions can be accepted by the teacher, provided they are not too impractical. Such discussions have a distinct value, in that the reaching of some kind of broadly agreed decision is real, and imperative — it may not matter too much if our discussion about how to capture the Norman castle breaks down, but we really *need* decisions about the village frieze before we can start. The force of this message about the real-life value of discussion is doubled, of course, if the decisions are actually accepted honestly by the teacher, and if the teacher avoids the temptation to manipulate the discussion. The easiest way to avoid that temptation, of course, is to try so far as possible to have such decision-making discussion take place in small groups with the teacher taking no active part in any group.

Evaluating Discussion

The implications for evaluation of this approach to discussion are two-fold. We can evaluate, as it were, the products of discussion, the responses to some problem, say, in the same way as we evaluate an individual response, i.e. in terms of how well supported it is by reasoning, how many aspects of the problem are taken on board, and whether there is evidence of tentativeness in the conclusion. Secondly, we can attempt to evaluate something much more elusive, the quality of the discussion itself. One aspect of discussion quality is not too difficult to evaluate, and that is the actual number of child-to-child, as opposed to child-to-teacher, exchanges, which take place. We can feel encouraged if such exchanges take place at all, above the level of 'Shut up!' or 'That's daft!' As to the quality of such exchanges though, or indeed as to the quality of what children say to the teacher, in practice our judgement will have to be impressionistic unless we are prepared to make and analyse tape recordings. At the level of impressions, though, we can listen for instances of the following sorts of behaviour, illustrated in this truncated version of a discussion on 'shops'.

Child A: I like the Co-op best, they've got all sorts, all the stuff in one shop. (giving reasons for statements)
Child B: I like Fine Fare.
Teacher: Yes.
Child A: Miss, if you live at a shop do you get the things . . . free? (asking questions)
Teacher: Does anybody know?
Child A: Carl lives at B——s (a corner shop).
Child C: My dad lets me have things but we still have to pay the man
(Carl)   when they come.
Child D: I'd like to live at a fish shop.
Child A: Yes . . . but you'd get fed up.
Teacher: What sort of shop would be best to have?
Child D: A fish shop.
Child A: A sweet shop would be good. But might it be better so you could get more sensible things free like a . . .? (tentativeness)
Child B: You might be sick if you ate sweets all day.
Child D: A garage would be better, you could get . . . er . . . cars and petrol. (change of opinion, possibly influenced by A?)

Giving reasons, asking questions, tentativeness of response and, above all, signs of actually listening to other people and modifying one's views as a result, are the four principal marks of someone who is taking part in a 'good' discussion. They are elusive things to spot, in the ebb and flow of young children's talk, but at least if we know we are looking for them, we can form a broad impression as to whether they are actually increasing in frequency as a result of our teaching strategies for discussion, or not.

Children Talking: Drama

In their book *The Drama of History* (New University Education, 1974),
John Fines and Raymond Verrier give some descriptions of drama-work
with quite young children which have become, as it were, classic texts
for those interested in the teaching of history. What they have to say is
of equal relevance to non-historians interested in the broad field we have
designated as 'social studies', and might be briefly summarised under
three heads.

First and foremost, they stress that drama as an activity can and
should have very distinct learning goals, as well as general goals of the
order of 'self-expression'. One lengthy sequence they describe is very
overtly directed to the clarification and exploration of the concept of
'authority', another deals quite explicitly with the nature and problems
of historical evidence. Their second point arises from this main argument, i.e. that polished 'performance', elaborate props and dressing up
are not necessary in drama which has these kinds of goals — drama to
illuminate some aspect of 'topic' work is not the same animal as play-
production, though as Fines and Vernier point out:

> On some drama occasions the teacher may need clothes to help
> children into a role: a long robe may just sufficiently hamper the
> movements of the King as to remind him that he is the King . . .
> Similarly, hats may sometimes help younger children to hold them-
> selves in a character that might otherwise slip . . .

Thirdly, they note the close relationship of drama and discussion —
discussion occurs sometimes as an essential lead-in to drama — before
trying to act out the response of a group of Plains Indians to the
advent of white men, it is as well to discuss what sort of white men
might be the first to encounter Plains Indians, and the question of
whether all Indians, young, old, chiefs and non-chiefs, women and men,
would feel alike about the white intruders. Without this sort of
preliminary discussion we have the following sort of 'drama' which it
has been the misfortune of many, many teachers to witness.

1st White Man:	'We want to take your land!'
Indian:	'No you can't!' (stabs white man)
2nd White Man:	'Bang!' . . .

Discussion is also necessary at the end of drama sessions, for the children to consider, and the teacher, incidentally, to evaluate, what the drama has taught the children, what further issues and difficulties have been thrown up by the experience. This area, in fact, is one where the idea of children fruitfully holding as it were genuine, *necessary* discussion to plan the course and shape of their own work is particularly applicable.

As with drama, so with all of the activities we have discussed under this chapter heading 'Indirect Approaches'; they will always be more difficult to evaluate than more straightforward approaches, and there will always be the danger of them turning into agreeable time-fillers. But with a clear idea of what their learning objectives and outcomes might be, there is no reason at all why they should not be both very useful and also capable of being evaluated in a reasonably rigorous way.

Notes on Exercises

Exercise 1 – Suggestions

The question 'Why is x where it is?', i.e. explaining the reasons for a site would be useful in very many cases, though it is worth remembering that the reasons for the siting of many castles is no longer as obvious today as when they were built. The question about 'who is the most important person' will likewise be useful in almost any situation involving a hierarchy of authority. Another interesting question is 'who gets paid the most?', and yet another variant, in the case of people with mysterious titles like 'manager' is 'what exactly does he do?' Any shop must have means, however discreet, of persuading people to buy, and we would enquire how that persuading is done, similarly the management of any factory must have decided to produce goods of a certain type, size, colour or whatever, and this could be investigated (how do Raleigh decide what colour to spray their bikes, why does the TV factory make mostly 16″ screen sets, and so on). Any workplace must contain people who learned to do the jobs they are doing – how did they learn them, how long did it take?

'What would happen if . . .' style questions might be put directly to people, as say 'what happens if the conveyor belt breaks down' or 'if you needed an extra helper in the shop, what would you do?'

This question type, or variants of it, can be useful in the case of, say, castles, where we make the children themselves work out the answer. The most obvious case would be, 'how would you attack the castle?' Making the children refer to real physical features, and if they can, approximate dimensions (e.g. of a moat), and getting them to produce a sketch-diagram to illustrate their answer, can provide most interesting and thought-provoking conflicts and contrasts with their answers to the flatter, more abstract 'how might you attack a castle' type of question set, as a preliminary exercise, back at school.

PART THREE

PLANNING AND EVALUATION

8 LEVELS OF DIFFICULTY

John is described by his teacher as a bright child. What exactly, we may ask the teacher, makes him decide that John is outstanding in the group? Clearly John is successful at the tasks set, but we need to observe and describe his behaviour precisely and specifically if we are to know how to cater not only for him but also for Richard described as 'rather slow'.

'Quick' and 'slow', at one level, are accurately used as adjectives descriptive of children's abilities. If the children in the class are all set the same work John who is 'quick' finishes early. Richard who is 'slow' may not have finished copying the title of the work set and the day's date. In John's case therefore he needs much more to do. A wise teacher will always have some further task for 'early finishers' who otherwise might waste time or, bored, cause disciplinary problems by finding their own time-filling but anti-social activities. If Richard has so little drive it is also a mistake to let him dissipate his energy on copying out an elaborate title or, as is sometimes the practice – a wasteful one we think – copying out the question he has to answer from the board or from a book.

Children like Richard may find the mechanics of writing a struggle. While it is agreed they need practise to improve their skills, it is a good idea to separate practice in mechanical writing skills from tasks which require thought. A one word answer may well indicate perfectly well that Richard has understood a question and can answer it relevantly. For instance: Q. If you were shipwrecked on a desert island, what is the main thing you would need? A. Fire.

One word answers to questions are perfectly acceptable in the everyday world, but some teachers think it necessary to require children to put their answers in formal sentences every time. It may be wise to ask the slow children to do this occasionally but not always for it holds them up and may be very discouraging. Another way of providing for the individual speeds of children in a class is to produce work-cards which begin with simple questions and become progressively more difficult, finishing with an open-ended task which allows the abler children to write at some length. For instance a work-card which began with requiring a simple observation of everyday life – 'What work does your dad do?' might proceed to require the child to make a judgement

'Is his work hard?' and finish with the open-ended task 'Draw a picture to show two of the different jobs done in this school and in each picture show what tools or equipment are used in each job.'

When student teachers are asked to study examples of children's written work and decide which is the best and which the worst, they are often very much influenced by the children's handwriting and by their literary skills, i.e. their ability to use capital letters and full stops, and to write well-formed sentences. It is very likely that John our 'bright' child writes legibly and has mastered the skill of writing in sentences and that Richard, the child classed by his teachers as 'slow', forms his letters crudely, begins sentences with 'And' and may even leave out the essential verb altogether. It is possible however to be led by a child's poor literary skills to underestimate his intellectual ability. Look at picture G – the handwriting is nearly illegible. This child, however, in a unit of which work led to a discussion of unemployment due to technological change, was able to suggest the retraining of the redundant workers at 'skill centres'. In other words his capacity for thought was much greater than his teacher, conditioned by the sight of his spidery scrawl, expected.

A further difference between John and Richard is the size and nature of the vocabulary of each child. This is particularly important since language is a moderately faithful reflection both of conceptual level and of the range of experiences a child has enjoyed. The more able child has probably had a wider range of experiences than the less able child and, from this range of experiences, concepts have been formed. For example, John may have visited not one harbour but several: it is all the easier for him to use the word accurately in an appropriate context and to draw a map of an imaginary island so that it includes a harbour. Richard, less fortunate, may not even have seen a picture showing a harbour and when the word occurs in a story may have trouble reading it. He certainly would not introduce it spontaneously into conversation or writing. He is however quite happy with words like 'ship' which represent concrete objects he *has* seen. It is the higher level of abstraction, where language is applied to complex groups of things (like 'harbour') or to matters remote from his personal experience, which gives him trouble.

Differences in vocabulary affect reading ability. The more able child reads more fluently, has a larger reading vocabulary and is often willing to spend more time reading for information or pleasure than the less able. The abler child too has a series of related reading skills, he knows alphabetical order which enables him to use indices or encyclopedias, he can select what he wants from a table of contents, and is not thrown if the information obtained from two different books is different in emphasis. For the less able child a densely printed book or work-sheet is in itself disheartening since for him, as yet, reading is in itself a major task, not a useful instrument at his service for a range of purposes.

Picture G

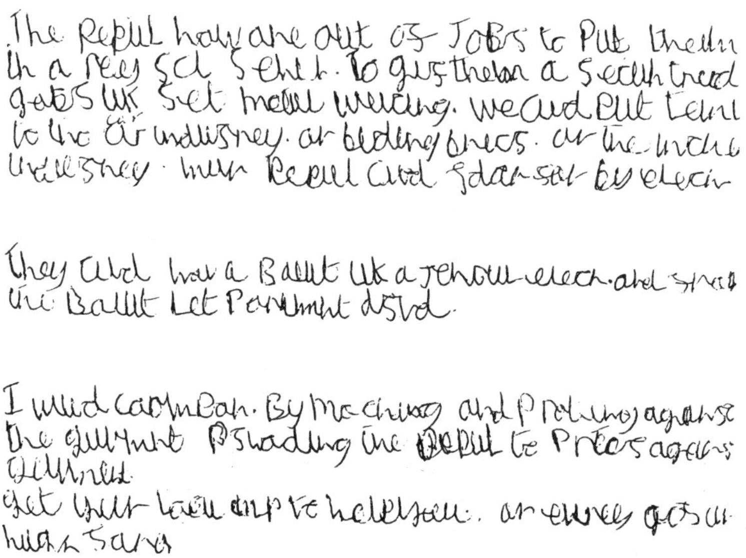

[handwritten text]

The people who are out of jobs to put them in a re-skill centre. To give them a second trade, jobs like sheet metal welding we could put them to the car industry or building bricks. At the machine industry more people could generate by electricity.

They could have a ballot like a general election and show the ballot. Let Parliament decide.

I would campaign. By marching and protesting against the government. Persuading the people to protest against government.

Get your local M.P. to help you or even go on hunger strike.

So far we have been discussing comparatively superficial differences between John and Richard, differences so superficial that it might well be that, given more propitious circumstances, Richard might prove as capable of understanding as John. If however we were to invite the two boys to tackle a question requiring conceptual understanding or the exercise of intellectual skill we might be able to say with confidence — and with evidence — John is the abler child. For example suppose we ask John and Richard 'Who is the most important person in the school?' John says, 'The headteacher is the most important person. She tells people what to do and they do it, and the children do it as well.' Here John has shown that he understands not only the concept of importance and can use it correctly but also understands something about the concept of power and may see the school as a society, though neither 'power' nor 'society' are as yet in his vocabulary. When Richard says, 'Mrs J. is most important. She cooks my dinner', Richard has some grasp of the concept of importance but his thinking is highly egocentric and 'concrete', as that of young children tends to be. He is intellectually less mature than John and probably understands a lot less about the concept of power. And in addition if we show both children a picture of Stone Age men and ask 'What do you think they are going to do next?' John may reply, 'They are going to hunt some animals, kill them with those weapons, then have a feast', while Richard says, 'They'll go home for their tea.' John has shown greater ability to extrapolate plausibly from the evidence in the picture and greater understanding than Richard.

In short, the touchstone is the ability to think and understand. This is a good deal more difficult to recognise than neat handwriting and we shall be addressing ourselves to this problem at length later in the chapter.

Student teachers often complain that some of their less able pupils have 'no interests'; this may well be because they do not have the interests inexperienced teachers expect or hope to find in children, such as interests in the accepted repertoire of primary school topics. It may however be true that the interests of less able children are less easily identified or when apparently aroused are shortlived. Compared to able children they have a markedly lower capacity to persist with even a self-imposed task without distraction, without the stimulus of early and frequent feedback in the form of success and praises and without changes in the nature of the activity. Able children can persist and, given an aroused interest in a field, can pursue more distant goals persistently.

Finally, it is a mistake to assume that children who have difficulty with academic work are necessarily more successful with practical or 'creative' activities. Ability is frequently characterised by success in a wide range of tasks especially in children under the age of thirteen. The less able child cannot be expected to be markedly more successful in work involving making a frieze of the village street. His pictures, especially those produced in the context of topic work, will not necessarily show a wealth of illustrative detail accurately reflecting an observed scene. Tasks of this kind may require the understanding of concepts like 'transport' or 'community' which characterise the able child or may require precise observation, an intellectual skill in itself.

Nevertheless, it would be wrong to suggest that the profile of an individual child's abilities may not contain inconsistencies. A child may be able to produce pictures which communicate his meaning more effectively than his compositions do. Children with reading difficulties are not necessarily stupid: indeed it is not impossible for a 'bright' child to conceal his problem with reading by closely paying attention to the spoken word and to pictures.

An even more disastrous mistake would be to assume that children from poor backgrounds are necessarily less able than children from affluent middle-class suburbs. It is perhaps astonishing that in 1981 we should find it necessary to make such a statement. The effect of some recent sociological work, e.g. that of Bernstein, has been unwittingly to reinforce the class prejudice which some students bring to the task of teaching. It is not unusual to hear a student teacher say – 'Of course this is a working class school and the children aren't very bright.' A complementary error has been demonstrated by teachers, who would consider themselves radicals and on the side of the working-class child, who have laid themselves open to the criticism that they are anti-intellectual, rejecting the importance of initiating the child into the culture on the grounds that it is bourgeois and searching for an alternative in the child's own neighbourhood.

In our opinion, we must assume that in any unstreamed primary school class in a working-class neighbourhood whether traditionally 'white' or with a substantial number of black children, there will be children of high intellectual potential who need the stimulus of an education which treats intellectual development as the central goal, and that in any affluent suburb there will be children of limited ability who also need an appropriate education. Furthermore, children of limited ability, whatever their background, are assumed to be capable of progress in understanding social, economic, even political, ideas.

Now we have stated the problem. John and Richard are not equally able members of families in the same societies, of the same peer group in the same school on the same estate of the same industrial town, but they are encountering similar challenges to their understanding. Our problem is how the understanding of each may be developed without either experiencing the frustration of a struggle with ideas too remote, or the corresponding frustration produced by what the Americans call 'Mickey Mouse'-type work of a low, undemanding level.

We have already, earlier in this chapter, introduced two methods of varying the level of difficulty. We suggested that teachers might consider very carefully the length and size of the task. They already do this of course when they provide a series of work-cards, perhaps five or six, instead of putting all the exercises on one card. This is very sensible because if the work is broken down in manageable units, the child receiving one card at a time is given a job he can imagine finishing and, having done it, has a sense of achievement and success which gives him the incentive to start a new card. If all his work were put on one sheet of paper, the last task on the sheet might seem discouragingly distant. Even adults can be disheartened by a string of instructions ending, 'And when you have done those, there is still A, B and C to do.'

Very often tasks, which appear to be single exercises, in fact embody a large number of different tasks; for example, 'Write a composition on . . .' and some children have trouble deciding where to begin. If in topic work on 'Birds' we said, 'Your job, Tony, is to find out about eagles', consider what is involved. Tony needs to use an encyclopedia and perhaps select several relevant books, scanning their contents and indices for references to eagles. He may need to find out where eagles are seen and look the places up in an atlas. And it needs a certain amount of general knowledge to know that he then needs to collect information about eagles' nests, eggs and breeding practices, their mode of flight, their prey, their method of catching it, and so on. Altogether it is a whole package of work to which he could apply himself for weeks. Even when a child is given a question, which we might assume would focus his attention more precisely, it may in fact turn out to be a portmanteau of questions. For example 'Why did the Indians hate the white man?' invites multiple responses and might be answered at very great length by a well-informed and enthusiastic child drawing on his reading and film-viewing experience.

It is a good rule therefore to look hard at the size of the task we are setting and, when a child is known to work slowly or can be seen to have difficulty, to shorten it. Instead of asking for a composition, we should ask for a paragraph or, if that term is unfamiliar, half a page; instead of asking for a paragraph we should perhaps ask the child to write one sentence. If we want to encourage children to practise giving multiple responses, i.e. lots of answers to a question, a very desirable ability to cultivate, why not ask them to make lists rather than write continuous prose, a demanding exercise which requires all their concentrated attention and may slow them down so much that they lose sight of the object that you had in mind. Listing rapidly is a most useful skill, it can be tackled by a group of children as a co-operative effort and, once familiar as a technique, can be practised in jotters, as a valuable preliminary before children are asked to produce a more polished version in sentences. One might say, for instance 'Make a list of the things you would find useful to take if you were starting life in this new land' or 'Write down as many words as you can describing how you would feel on starting at a new school'.

Where questions do not lend themselves so obviously to listing, they can often be broken down into their component parts and handled step by step. For example if the question is about transport, it can be broken down into aircraft, cars, trains, lorries and bicycles, roads and railways. The child who can do this breaking down exercise can easily pick out the logical headings of a series of paragraphs. In fact teachers can very usefully show children how portmanteau questions can be reduced to their component parts and then let children practice doing it themselves, either individually or in groups. They will be learning a useful technique which will stand them in good stead across the curriculum.

Sometimes the problem with a question is not only the multiplicity of sub-questions it contains, but also the language in which it is expressed. The instruction itself may be couched in unfamiliar academic terminology. As experienced teachers know we need to say to primary school children not 'Write an essay . . .' but 'Tell me about', not 'Classify' but 'Which of these go together?', not 'Account for . . .' but 'Why?', and 'What can we say about all these . . .' rather than 'Can we make a generalisation about these?' In other words we need to forget the language of 'O' and 'A' level examination papers and use simpler forms of words. We should remember perhaps that children are thought to respond better to a teacher whose speech is colloquial, than to those whose utterances are formally academic and therefore alien to the children and remote from their experience of conversations at home.

Often, however, the crucial difficulty for many children is the language of the question itself. Let us take for the purposes of illustration what may look like an extreme example —

   'How is the life of the *Bedouin adapted* to their *environment*?'

Here it appears that a child might have trouble with the words in italics. He might find them hard to read and even if he could read, then hard to understand. We can make the question easier if we replace 'Bedouin' by 'people'. Environment cannot be replaced so simply: by environment we mean the climate, the flora and fauna, the physical features. We can make the child's task shorter and easier if we consider one feature at a time, express it in language familiar to him and choose one well within his experience, e.g. the weather. So if we ask the child 'How are the people's lives adapted to the weather?, he may well be able to cope a good deal better.

   Even this modified question is substantial since people's lives can mean the lives of men, women, old and young and could cover food, clothing, homes, not to mention customs, beliefs and the economy. Although life is not a word even the most thoughtful teacher might think it necessary to explain to a child it can be used at a variety of levels, and in the context of this question means 'way of life' or even 'culture', very comprehensive and indeed difficult ideas that need taking to pieces in exactly the same way as 'environment'. Children therefore can be helped to cope with the question if they are asked to consider only one aspect of the life of the Bedouin — a familiar and concrete one such as 'clothes'. The question in its new form therefore is 'How are people's clothes adapted to the weather?' The notion of adaptation remains the chief outstanding difficulty and we can meet this by rephrasing the task 'How does the weather affect the sort of clothes people wear?' We can give further help and make the question still more specific and tell the child the kind of weather involved, 'How does the hot weather affect the sort of clothes people wear?'

   If we consider what we have done with this admittedly hard question we can see that we have broken it down into its component parts, and we have asked the pupil to answer only one part of the whole. In addition we have replaced highly abstract concepts by concrete examples of them. The vocabulary of the question has been made easier by excluding proper names. Throughout we have come nearer to children's experience. In changing the form of the question however we have not lost the understanding which the children are learning; whether they attempt the question in its simplest form or one of the more difficult versions, they are learning the idea that people's way of life is adapted to their environment and this is not beyond the grasp of even a seven-year-old child.

There is one further step we may need to take to help the understanding of Richard, the less able child. We can provide him with a picture which might show Eskimos in furs, Bedouins in white robes, Londoners in raincoats or spacemen in space suits. All these pictures could be used to promote the same understanding.

To sum up, to make a question easier for a less able child we shorten it, simplify the language, provide concrete examples of the more difficult/abstract notions, come nearer to children's experience and we provide supportive illustrations. What we do not do is give up the task of developing the understanding of the child by saying 'If you can't do it Richard, draw the picture instead.'

On page 128 we provide examples of tasks to be made shorter and easier by applying the principles outlined above. Take particular care however to look out for words which because they are short and familiar look 'easy' but conceal hidden difficulties, as we saw the word 'life' did. And not all concepts can be taken apart in exactly the same way. If we take the question 'Why did they rebel?', 'rebel' is short for quite a complex range of activities and what is needed is an example, 'Why did they refuse to do as they were told?', 'Why did they attack the king?' or 'Why did the men disobey the boss?' Each of these circumlocutions tells the learner more about the situation and therefore provides him with clues to the answer and some of the words he needs to use in his reply. Other 'deceptive' words include 'difference' and 'important'. Even straightforward words can become 'deceptive' in certain contexts; 'strong' is a very good example. Try, first, explaining to a group of junior children what a 'strong' castle might be like. Then try explaining the sentence 'William was a strong king' and it soon becomes clear that in the second case 'strong' is, in fact, a shorthand for some rather difficult ideas.

At the other end of the spectrum are words which are remote from children's vocabulary, though the ideas they incorporate are not entirely outside their experience. An example of this might be 'justice' — not a term which springs to the lips of a seven-year-old though he will be quick to say 'It's not fair . . .' In this and similar cases we need what Marion Blank calls a verbal mediator. Instead of using the words power or authority, again not often found in the spoken vocabulary of our classes, we can say 'Who tells people what to do?' 'Telling people what to do' becomes a useful mediator for power and can be used as a substitute for it until pupils acquire and use the words power and authority. Other useful verbal mediators include 'Can we vote about it? What could we have votes about?' Exercise 4 on page 129 asks you to find verbal mediators for a number of other words of this kind.

Earlier in this chapter, we suggested a different way of raising the level of difficulty. This was first identified by the American curriculum theorist Hilda Taba, who recommends that in certain kinds of work, one starts at a low level of difficulty, by asking for the recall of an experience, e.g. 'What did they do?' 'What did you notice about the car?' 'What happened when they quarrelled?' This is a level at which all children can participate. The level of discussion can then be raised with questions requiring the use of other intellectual skills, for example:

(1) What does your dad do? (recall of experience)
Is the work hard? (evaluation)
What makes it hard? (requiring criteria for evaluation, long hours, night work, heat, etc.)

(2) What happened . . . (recall of experience)
Why do you think it happened like that? (interpretation)
What might have happened next? (extrapolation)

(3) What did you notice about the policeman's car? (recall of experience)
How does it work? (interpretation)

(4) How was he dressed? (recall of experience)
Why does he wear a uniform? (interpretation)
Is it a good thing policemen wear uniforms? (evaluation)

(5) What is the rule about X? (recall)
Why do we have this rule? (interpretation)

This process is something many experienced teachers do intuitively but for many of us it helps to make the intuitive fully conscious and deliberate. It is very worthwhile tape-recording your discussions with children so that you can see if you are in fact doing this already and if you can see occasions when you have missed the chance to raise the level. To review your handling of oral situations in this way is very valuable for improving your teaching skills. Furthermore, if you accustom children to doing this orally you can then ask them to do it in written assignments. While the less able children may only be able to 'raise the level' once, more able children should soon learn to pursue a sequence of questions involving a range of different skills. For example:

What do they do?

Why do you think they do it?
Was it a good thing to do?
What makes you think so?
If you were (specify a situation) what would you do?
How do you think they felt about X?
Have you ever felt like that?
Why do you think they felt that way?

Where children have difficulty with questions that require the use of such intellectual skills, we have a rather different problem. Suppose the learner has answered the questions 'What does your dad do?' and 'Is it hard?' but cannot say what makes his Dad's work hard, we can help him by providing clues in the form of supplementary questions 'Are the hours long? Does he work shifts? Is it a dirty job? Does he have to carry heavy things?' What in fact we are doing for the child here is to 'unwrap' the concept of 'hard work'. At the end he should have some understanding not only as to whether his father works hard but also greater understanding of the concept of work. Providing clues in this case is not just making it easy, but providing necessary supplementary teaching. Similarly a child encountering the question 'How did you feel about X?', may be at a loss for the language to express himself. The teacher can provide a series of adjectives from which he can select, anxious, nervous, excited, ashamed, amused, bored etc.

There are a number of other tasks where some children may find 'clues' helpful. Where learners are given a picture and are asked the question 'Are these people rich or poor?', the clues in the picture indicating the people are poor may be the bare feet of the mother, the thinness of the child and the shelter of boxes built on the pavement of the Indian city. In these circumstances if a learner hesitates, one may say 'Why are they living on the pavement?' 'Is their house as comfortable as yours?' 'Why don't they have any shoes?' In this way we are drawing attention to the clues in the picture.

This technique is useful in most cases where children are practising intellectual skills. For instance if we are asking children to extrapolate as in this question: 'What would have happened to the Normans if the English had won?' We may add such questions as 'Who would have run away?' 'Where would they go?' 'What would the English do?' Again if we ask children to distinguish between innate and learned behaviour many teachers would suggest that this task, drawn from the discipline of psychology, was wholly outside children's range. But suppose we say, 'Richard has a puppy who is 10 weeks old. Which of these things will he need to teach the puppy? Barking, walking on a lead, burying bones in the ground, coming when called, growling, wagging his tail, sleeping', even young primary school children can sort out which is 'innate' and which 'learned' in this context. All they lack is the language to describe it. In ways like this we can make apparently difficult ideas easier. The brighter child can be stretched by being introduced to the new word 'innate' and be encouraged to use it, the less able need not be bothered with it just yet if it seems inappropriate, and we can often help the slower child by providing him with props that quicker children may not need. If children are to be asked to write a written report either of a visit or a summary of information collected on a particular topic, we can discuss the chief headings to be used and put them on the blackboard. For example, if the topic is an explorer, the headings might be:

Why he went.
What he took.
His problems.
What he found.

You will notice we have expressed these in language which children might use. It is best if they suggest the headings so that they may gradually learn this useful way of working. Now try Exercise 6 (page 129). Even so, children like Richard may be better employed in answering, say, three questions instead of trying to compose an essay. The questions will ensure they get the material in the right order and help them to avoid going off at a tangent. On 'Explorers' the questions might be:

Why did X go on his journey?
How did he travel?
What made the journey hard?
Where did he go?

In 'problem' situations the level of difficulty is determined by the number of variables involved. We think that as a general rule children in the concrete operational stage can cope with four variables at a time, but this is a very crude distinction since the variables themselves may be near to children's experience or more remote from it. Certainly we raise the level of difficulty by increasing the variables involved. For example, if children were asked to choose a place to cross the road they might have to consider one variable only: a bend in the road which obscured visibility. It would be therefore a fairly easy task to choose a place where visibility was good. But if in addition to the bend there were other hazards, say parked cars and a hill which also obscured visibility, the child would have to chose a place taking into consideration all three hazards. Less able children, unable to cope with three variables at once, may pay attention to only one of these conditions at a time. In any task involving maps or models where children are asked to make a decision, such as where to put a children's playground, or where to build a castle, the teacher can manipulate the number of variables according to the children's level of ability. In the case of the castle, the variables to be considered might be hills, river, tracks, water supply; in the case of an airport, distance from the nearest city, railway, motorway, site of great natural beauty, houses where people will be disturbed by the aircraft, etc; in the case of a playground, proximity to traffic, etc.

Some types of simulation involve a rather different kind of problem solving – problems involving human behaviour. For example in the process of teaching ideas like 'democracy', 'power' and 'justice', we might postulate the problem of the control of the television set. 'John wants to watch football. So does Dad. But Mary says "Why can't we have the Muppets . . ." ' The children are asked to suggest possible solutions: Father decides; they take turns; there is a vote; the time is shared between the two programmes, etc. The task of the children is to list all possible solutions, choose the best solution and give reasons for their choice. Apart from the intrinsic value of the exercise the children are learning a useful problem-solving technique which we hope they will transfer to other situations. In this case the less able children will produce a longer list of possible solutions if they work co-operatively as a group; they can then make and defend their individual choice of the best decision. More independent, able children can be asked to work alone from the beginning.

In some cases we can vary the complexity of the human problem especially where a choice is required. There is not much point in asking children to choose between obvious 'goodies' and obvious 'baddies': they need to learn the difficult task of choosing between shades of grey. So if we are asking them to choose the most suitable (imaginary) person to be a football captain we may give one sentence descriptions for the slower children. 'Richard is very good at scoring goals but does not always turn up for the game. John is a reliable boy who can run very fast. Philip is good-natured and loves football though he is not terribly good at it.' The more able children might choose between more possibilities and more substantial descriptions of more subtle characters — 'James is tall and strong. He is always good at ball games but apt to lose his temper if he isn't winning. He knows this is his main fault and is trying to get over it.'

Now, and not least important, we must consider the problem of children with very limited reading ability. With the younger children in the primary school something can be done by using pictures. For example we can devise picture sorting exercises to promote the skill of classification. Children can be asked to sort out pictures showing people working and those showing people playing. As they become more confident it is useful if some of them are ambiguous. Is a professional footballer playing or working? Similar exercises may involve choosing pictures showing rich and poor, people of today and long ago, farmers and hunters, England and 'far away'. We may ask children to pick out all the pictures representing transport, or different forms of power. In other words some moderately difficult concepts can be represented pictorially, e.g. in history, castles or sieges; in geography, deserts, jungles, the arctic, volcanoes, harbours, peninsulas, estuaries; in sociology, family, tribe, rituals like baptism and marriage. Children with reading difficulties may therefore be asked to match picture and caption in the context of topic work. More elaborate exercises with pictures may involve arranging events in sequence. This might be done not only with the events of a story, for sequencing in this way is a learned skill, but also with concepts like trade, agriculture, manufacture, mining where a process is involved. Young children could arrange in sequence pictures which showed the production of bread from the ploughing of the land to the purchase of the loaf or the building of a house from laying the foundation to painting and decorating. In the context of work on authority they could sort out pictures showing uniforms which indicated the person's identity, from pictures which showed uniforms indicating authority, and others showing uniforms whose chief function was to protect the wearer. If they found these groups overlapped or that some uniforms served a double or triple function, discussion might increase understanding usefully.

Similarly, not all drawing tasks need involve mindless copying (cf. chapter 7). If one says, in the context of the story of the Norman Conquest, 'draw me a picture of soldiers attacking', one is setting a task requiring the translation of a concept from one medium to another. With very young children beginning a topic on 'Work', one might say to all of them 'Draw a picture of someone you have seen working' and begin by discussing the different kinds of work they have observed. This can be a very illuminating test of the level of understanding of work which they have. Do they show tools? Have they got any notion of work in, say, a bank or an office or a factory or a mine, most of which they will not know from personal experience. To draw all the vehicles seen on the roads, rail and river and label them collectively 'transport' may be a useful reinforcement of a newly learned concept. In drawing tasks of this kind the addition of a written caption, however brief, is vital for the less able child and the caption should be devised by the child, even if help is needed with spelling and writing.

Tasks involving questions on pictures may be especially suitable for children with reading difficulties since they can often 'read' the picture and get a good deal of information from it; the written questions on it can be helpfully brief and simple and doubly easy to manage since the picture helps them to guess the content. It is a good idea to provide, possibly on the back of the picture, words they might need to answer the questions.

The matter of helping young readers by providing them with contextual clues, referred to in the section on 'Books', is obviously vitally important when the reader is a poor, hesitant one, and applies to the simplest piece of reading, like the following two examples.

He worked in the factory.
The factory where he worked . . .

Here the most unfamiliar word is probably 'factory'. In the first statement there is a clue as to its meaning in the first three words: it has to mean a place where people work and the child struggling to understand this new word knows he must be looking for a word, naming and describing the workplace. This narrows the field of choice: the unknown word has to be one of a very limited number of possible words. In the second statement however the new word comes at the beginning and there are no helpful clues introducing it. The clue to its meaning follows not precedes the new word, a situation initial readers find harder. The child struggling to decypher it knows that hundreds of words are preceded by 'the' and the field of choice is infinitely and dishearteningly wide.

So if we are using material about, say, a siege we start: 'The King put soldiers round the town. No-one was allowed to go in or out. The people in the town got hungry since the siege lasted a long time.' We do not start: 'The siege lasted a long time . . .' Now you might try to write a few lines with contextual clues in mind as suggested in Exercise

8 below.

Fluent readers become accustomed to looking ahead for contextual clues; hesitant ones may need to be taught specifically to scan a passage searching for them. In general, however, we need to write teaching materials for children bearing in mind the importance of meaning in the reading process.

Another device helpful to this particular group of children is to give them tasks where their reading ability is not unduly taxed. Where a project requires the collection of information they may be the ones asked to interview people. If they are to do this they will need help with this questionnaire and the teacher can assist them to devise questions answerable by Yes/No or by ticks and crosses or by numbers, with perhaps one open-ended question at the end. The children are likely to learn quite a lot in this way but the recording of the information will not be unduly taxing. This kind of thing might be part of a topic on work where people are interviewed about their jobs. 'Do you like your job? Is it hard? Did you have to be trained to do it? How long was your training? How old were you when you started to learn it? Did you get it through the Labour Exchange? Do you tell other people what to do?' etc. The data accumulated by the children could easily be recorded also in non-verbal ways, e.g. by the use of a graph to show the number of 'yes' responses to particular questions.

Exercises

Exercise 1

Break down the following tasks into their component parts.
(1)   Find out about Red Indians.
(2)   What happens when volcanoes erupt?

Exercise 2

Make up some listing exercises to be used in the context of a topic on 'shops'.

Exercise 3

Try to make these tasks and questions easier:
(1)   What can be done to improve transport in your area?
(2)   Make a map of the neighbourhood.
(3)   What makes things grow?
(4)   How does a car work?

(5) What are the causes of pollution?
(6) Why do fish die in the river?
(7) What makes the air smoky?

Exercise 4

Find verbal mediators for manufacturer, traitor, local government, evidence.

Exercise 5

Look at picture H. Devise one major question on it for the abler child. Then think up some questions which might draw the less able child's attention to the relevant clues.

Picture H

Exercise 6

Devise appropriate headings for a child's report on the following subjects:
(1) A visit to a castle.
(2) How we made an aquarium.
(3) Our street a hundred years ago.

Exercise 7

Devise a task involving a decision about where to put a castle involving:
(a) two variables;
(b) four variables.

Exercise 8

Write a few lines incorporating the new word: mammal. Then try: invasion, tribes, colony.

Exercise 9

Make up a questionnaire for use by children with limited literacy in the context of topic work on either 'shops' or 'our street' or 'in Grandma's day'.

9 EVALUATING CHILDREN'S WORK

Peter, aged 10, has been working on the following set of tasks (five interpretation and one evaluation), based on a picture of a medieval castle and on a brief discussion about castles.

(1) Why were castles built?
(2) Why did castles have high walls?
(3) Why does the castle in the picture have narrow slots in the wall?
(4) Why is the castle on a big mound?
(5) What is the portcullis for?
(6) Is it a good idea to have towers on both sides of the gate?

His answers are as follows:

(1) Castles were built to look afder land so the land does not get tacune.
(2) Castles have high walls so the enirmy can not climb over the wall.
(3) Lots of castles narrow slots so they shoot a arrow at the enirmy.
(4) Lots of casles wir bilt on mounds. So they can fight better.
(5) Portcullis are for if the enirmy gets past the drawbridge they wonte get past the portcullis.
(6) the castle gate had towers both side so if the enirmy trise smash the drawbridge they can shoot the enirmy with a arrow.

As teachers, we have to evaluate this response in various ways, asking ourselves questions like: 'Does this response show understanding? Does it show progress? Would it have been better to set a different task?' All these questions must be answered eventually but first and most pressingly we have to evaluate it for Peter's benefit, in language he will understand, in ways which will show him clearly how to improve and above all, in ways which will encourage him to go on working and succeeding.

It is a good idea, when faced with children's work, always to look first for something specific to praise. In this case, let us assume that these answers do not represent any sudden leap forward by Peter, but rather his average standard of work, so our 'feedback' to him could begin with modest praise, something like 'Good. You've thought about all the questions, and you've thought carefully especially about number 6'. This praise is reasonable, and more likely to be effective than a blanket, uninformative 'Good', or than a negative comment such as 'Too many careless mistakes in spelling'.

But what about the spelling and other shortcomings? When we come to point these out, it is vital that we are both precise and constructive. Stock terms of dis-praise such as 'careless' are unhelpful and often, in fact, untrue even as descriptions of the work. If we look for instance at how, in answer number 1, 'castles were built' becomes, in number 4 'casles wir bilt', then Peter's eagerness to get on, or boredom with a task that is too easy, or pressure of time, could all account for the reversion to a sort of phonetic spelling more adequately than the unhelpful idea of 'carelessness'. In the case of the spelling mistakes in these answers, it would be much the most useful course to show Peter how to spell just one or two important common words which he clearly cannot spell at the moment – 'enemy' is an obvious candidate plus, possibly, 'taken' ('tacune' in number 1). To learn to spell one or two new words will be more use to Peter than possibly unjust exhortations to 'Take more care about spelling'.

As to the content of the answers themselves, we could criticise number 1 as being a bit vague, number 4 could profitably tell us a lot more about the advantages of mounds, and number 6 is not phrased as an *evaluative* answer at all, as well as leaving us puzzled about why the enemy would be trying to 'smash' the drawbridge. Of these short-comings in the substance of the work the answer to number 4 might be the best to take up with Peter, because we could handle it relatively simply. We could say something like 'Yes, that's right. Can you say a bit more about how they could fight better, being high up on a mound.' The three important points in this remark are that the criticism is legitimately led into by a bit of praise ('Yes, that's right') and that the way for Peter to improve his answer, by expanding the idea 'fight better', is quite clear, and clearly hinted at by the phrase 'high up'.

If we have more time to spend with Peter's work, either marking it at home or talking to him about it in class, then we could take up answers 1 and 6, trying to (i) emphasise the good points of the existing answer; (ii) make absolutely clear where the shortcoming lies; (iii) give some clue as to how the improvement required might be made. (How might that be done in the case of those two answers, numbers 1 and 6?)

If we are, however, as usual, pressed for time, it is a good strategy to pick out *one* response, like number 4, where we can fairly easily give clear, constructive advice, and concentrate on that.

Exercise 1

Using the principles just outlined, try to put together a brief comment of not more than two or three sentences, on the following set of answers by Jeanne (10) to the same six questions answered by Peter:

(1) To gaurd the land of the people.
(2) High walls so you could not get over someone with a ladder.
(3) To look out of.
(4) To make it hard to clime up and get in the castle way.
(5) It is the gate.
(6) Yes so you could see who was coming to the gate and stop them getting in and somewhere to put the drawbridge down.

Exercise 2

Here are three short pieces of continuous prose by nine-year-olds, arising out of a visit to a castle, to be marked. The third presents the problem of highly incompetent work (which in the original was compounded by very ill-formed handwriting).

(1) (Lester)
     at the castle we saw was high wlls so peple cold see a long way and thick sts to to keep peple out it was on a big hill but i think not too big so peple cold get in if if attackrs.
(2) (Julie)
     We saw a castle on our nice trip. There had very thick walls and towers at the corners. The Keep was norman it was in the middle and there were other towers. The rest of it is forteenth century. The castle is on the hill to be on the best place. There is a nice car park.
(3) (John)
     The castel is nice and
     The castel is good wen I wur the castel it was mene people ther and it was nowing today but then
     and it was good and the we had went back home.

If we return now to the questions on castles set to Peter and Jeanne and their answers, we could say that, at least in the case of those two children, the whole activity might well on the face of it have had educational value. They have answered all the questions, all their answers are

at least adequate and sensible, and there is no sign of either of them
being out of their depth with excessively difficult ideas. Similarly, with
the work on the castle-visit by Lester, Julie and John, it is only John
who offers no observations on the castle as such, but only on the 'trip'
as an experience. However, we need to ask ourselves some hard questions before we can move beyond saying that most of the children
made a reasonable shot at the set tasks, to saying that the experiences
the children had and work they did were worthwhile, valuable, and
successful in the sense of bringing about worthwhile, appropriate
learning and progress. It is the process of formulating and answering
these questions which constitutes "evaluation" in its wider sense, and a
painful process it can be, as well as being an absolutely essential one.

The first question we might ask ourselves, is, what exactly was the
teacher trying to get the children to learn? In the case of Peter and
Jeanne the six questions posed clearly aim at developing the skills of
interpretation and evaluation, and might also be said to be aimed at
developing the concept 'castle'. The two learning processes are very
closely related, but for convenience and clarity we should separate
them, to consider the questions of 'developing' skills and 'developing'
concepts.

Evaluating Progress in Skills

The first five of Peter and Jeanne's questions involve interpretation, and
answering interpretation questions well might be divided into five main
stages, as follows:

Stage A. A child might be unwilling to address the question at all, might
not in fact be familiar with the idea that answers to questions can be
arrived at by processes other than recall of teacher's words or looking
up in a book. Intelligent children of junior age may need encourag-
ment to pass out of this stage if they have been accustomed only to
topic work involving copying/paraphrasing books. (It can be even more
difficult to prise children out of Stage A with even more unfamiliar
skills such as evaluation or extrapolation.)

Stage B. The child makes interpretations, but they are of the nature of
guesses, rather than appearing to be based on much reasoning, as if a
child said in response to number 5 (not as a joke) that the portcullis
was to let air into the castle. Actually, the 'portcullis' question is not a

good example at this point, since the portcullis' function is somewhat obvious, but question 1 'Why were castles built' could well yield Stage B answers such as 'For the people to live in' which would show the child not understanding that people do not usually build enormous, complex buildings just to 'live in'.

Stage C. Peter's 'portcullis' answer illustrates this stage very well – a simple, plausible interpretation, implying reasoning on his part, and showing that he has taken account in his reasoning of the whole situation of 'enemies', 'drawbridges' and attacks in which the particular thing to be 'interpreted' – the portcullis, is set.

Stage D. This stage involves children in making explicit the reasoning behind their interpretations. In question 4 ('Why is the castle on a big mound'), a better answer than Peter's might be: 'You would get extra height, so you would see the enemy coming sooner. Also if you dropped rocks or spears on the enemy they would fall harder, and the enemy would find it more difficult to throw their weapons up. So you would be better off in lots of ways.' This answer is longer than Peter's original response, but not *merely* longer. 'So they can fight better, and win, and drive the enemy off' would also be longer but would still not have the key characteristic of a Stage D answer – the element of explanation of how the basic response 'So they can fight better', was arrived at.

Stage E. This stage can be reached by junior children, though even adults find it difficult. If we answered question 1, 'Why were castles built', in a Stage E style, we would say something like: 'On the one hand, they might have been built by local rulers to protect their wealth from the local peasants, and generally scare the locals. On the other hand, their main function could have been to protect the local people from outside raiders, bandits, etc. They could even have had both purposes, it's really rather difficult to say.' In Stage E we demonstrate what Bruner and others call 'tentativeness', that is, a willingness to accept, even welcome, uncertainty. This is a sign that we are truly educated, in that we see questions as an invitation to seek the truth, rather than close the matter down with an 'answer'. The main difficulty in attaining Stage E is probably a matter of attitude and culture, rather than sheer intellectual difficulty, because so much of our learning, from pre-school to higher education, seems to be about getting right answers, not about registering well-founded doubt.

If we look now at the first five answers of Peter and Jeanne, in the light of our five-part breakdown of the skill of interpretation, we can say that all five of Peter's answers are C type. Jeanne's (Exercise 1) are likewise mostly C, though answer number 3 might be on the borderline of B. We can also note a very important feature of the questions themselves. Questions 1 and 4 offer the children the chance to give D, even E style answers, but in the case of 2, 3 and 5 it would be merely stilted and arguably pointless to go beyond a C answer. Take the case of number 5 — we could give an E answer and say: 'From its position in relation to what seems to be the gateway, the portcullis appears to be a sort of fortified gate. On the other hand, it might be a purely decorative feature — but on balance, it is likely to have the function of a fortified gate.' We could give such an answer, but it would be a waste of time, since the portcullis question is only *worth* a C-type response. The point is, that when we evaluate children's progress in skills, we also are evaluating the questions or tasks we are setting and, if our goal is to lead a child beyond C type answers up to more discursive and tentative responses, we obviously have to set tasks where that kind of response is both possible and sensible — otherwise we may fall into the trap of the young student-teacher who sought to achieve Bruner's ideal of tentativeness at a stroke by coaching her class to begin all their answers with 'Perhaps . . .', eliciting, thus, responses like: 'Perhaps the animal the Knight is riding is a horse.'

On a more serious note, what we can say with fair confidence about Peter and Jeanne is they both seem to operate at level C of the skill of interpretation with reasonable facility, but do not take the chances offered to go on to D type answers, and need prompting and encouragement to do so.

Question 6 invites the children to *evaluate* the plan of having flanking towers at gateways.

With the skill of evaluation, we might discern four stages of progress:

Stage A, unwillingness to try to respond.
Stage B, 'Yes' or 'No' judgements, unsupported by reasons.
Stage C, Judgements supported by reasons.
Stage D, Tentative judgements — 'on the one hand . . . on the other'.

Peter, interestingly, appears to be at Stage 'A', in that he does not offer an evaluation at all, but simply explains why flanking towers were built. Jeanne, on the other hand offers a 'C'-type answer, a judgement supported by reasons. This may genuinely show that Peter does not understand

what is required, or it may be that he read the work-sheet inattentively
– the important thing is that although on the whole his work is more
impressive than Jeanne's, this one response is the clearest signal in
either of the two sets of answers of a serious lack of comprehension,
and that this possibly serious blind spot could easily be obscured by the
general vigour of his response, and by factors such as his spelling errors,
unless we strictly evaluate his sixth answer as a response to a particular
kind of question.

The principal intellectual skills not represented in Peter and Jeanne's
work are translation, extrapolation, classification, synthesis and analysis.
Progress in the skill of translation, as a skill, is often difficult to measure, as this exchange shows:

Teacher: In the book it says about the soldiers, the Egyptians had what
          we call a 'regular' army. Do you know what that means?
Terry: They always have enough . . . they always have another defence
          if some go home.
Shirley: They always had a hundred. They always know how many
          they've got.

Clearly, it is very difficult here to separate the children's difficulty in
grasping the concept 'regular army' from their facility or otherwise in
'translating' the abstraction, i.e. expressing their understanding of the
idea. In keeping track of a child's progress in this area, it would be better
not to try to use A-E progress scales but to note progress in grasp of
concepts (see below, p. 140) and subsume ability to 'translate' in that.

With the skill of extrapolation, a four-part scale can be constructed,
very similar to the one applied to evaluation, going from Stage A,
unwillingness to try to respond, through three stages nicely illustrated
by these 8/9 year olds' answers to the question 'What would happen if
there were no policemen?'.

'Firse (fires) and crashs of cars.' (Stage B, i.e. genuine extrapolations,
but rather wild and not particularly logical)
'Peple cold do robberys and not get caght.'
'Crimes and murders and anything you likd to do.' (Stage C –
plausible extrapolations)
'Nobody wold be in het street to guide the cars so ther wold be
acidents.' (Stage D – plausible, argued extrapolation with reasons)
'Ther would be blazes and murders burglars, everybody would get
ther own you then somebody else mought by poliss or every body

will Die.' (This apocalyptic vision offers the germ of a Stage E, tentative extrapolation — *either* a sort of vigilante police would be formed *or* society will collapse)

The skill of classifying can likewise be divided into four stages of progress — moving from A, unwillingness to respond, through four stages very like those already applied to the skill of evaluating. These oral answers to the question put to six-year-olds 'Does going to school count as work', illustrate the point:

Stage B — 'Yes' (unsupported assertion).
Stage C — 'No we do work at school but we don't get any money because we're too young. It is work to learn not work to earn'. (Reasoned, argued response).
Stage D — not exemplified in this particular exchange would be the tentative stage, pointing out say, that school is "work" in some ways but not in others.

In exercise 2 (page 133) Lester, Julie and John are asked to write continuous prose, that is to *synthesise* the answers to a number of questions — questions either hinted at by the teacher ('Remember to mention the high walls') or left to the children themselves to work out by a process of *analysis*.

Success and failure at synthesis and analysis are very difficult to describe or analyse precisely. Work like John's induces despair in teachers, and makes us use language like 'a mess' 'formless' 'illiterate' and the like. It would, however, be very useful if we could quantify progress in these two skills, however crudely, especially in view of their great importance in schooling generally, as well as in topic work.

The simplest way is to tackle *analysis* first. In a 'good' answer this teacher might have required the following to be accounted for and awarded: One point for a mention, one for an explanation

(i) The site on a hill.
(ii) The thick walls.
(iii) The height of the walls.
(iv) The collapsed and waterless condition of the moat.
(v) He also required mention of the building dates of the castles. (one point)

Lester *mentions* the first three of these, so 'scores' three points. In each case he goes beyond mentioning to *explaining* the phenomena, so he gets three more points giving a total of 6. Julie mentions thick walls and mentions and accounts for the hill site, so far scoring 3 points. She mentions the building dates (1 point). She also mentions towers, the central position of the keep and the car park, and we now have to judge whether or not these extra things are relevant, and so earn 'bonus points', or irrelevant, incurring 'penalty points'. It would be reasonable to add two points for towers and keep, and take one off for the car-park — Julie's total, therefore, is 5.

This is a very crude way of answering the question 'Have these children understood what the exercise is all about, have they analysed the task correctly?', but it is much more useful than merely feeling that Lester is interesting, but a bit illiterate, and that Julie writes nicely but sometimes misses the point. And most important of all, it will enable us to keep track of a child's progress in analysis over the year, at least to the extent of noting whether or not there is an upward movement in the scores or not.

There is a large subjective element in evaluating progress in our last skill, *synthesis*. For some people, Lester's piece would be judged better than Julie's. It addresses the questions of walls (height), walls (thickness), and hill-site very pithily, without a wasted word, and it works in very neatly the idea of the hill being 'high but not too high'. Julie's on the other hand is written in sentences, has a formal introductory sentence and these virtues, for some teachers, would outweigh its rambling quality and make it a better piece of synthesis, of 'putting together', than Lester's. When we compare both pieces with John's, however, we can see that neither of them contains repetition, on the lines of John's: 'The castle is nice . . . the castle is good . . . and it was good'; neither of them contain false starts, like John's: 'The castle is nice and . . . The castle is good', and in all three cases, including John's, it is possible to tell at first reading what the piece is about. These three points, which might be summarised as lack of unnecessary repetition, coherence, and clarity of theme might offer a basic means of evaluating children's powers of synthesis, and have the extra merit of being not too difficult to communicate to children.

We might sum up generally on evaluating progress in skills as follows. interpretation and extrapolation can be seen as moving through five broadly defined stages; evaluation, extrapolation and classification through four stages. We could record a child's progress in these skills with some precision, C for example meaning that a child operates consistently at C level, C/D indicating that the child sometimes operates spontaneously at D level, and some symbol like C-D might be used to show the child can work at D level but always has to be prompted to do so.

The skill of analysis can be crudely evaluated by means of a points system, so that 50 per cent would mean that where a child has to analyse a task without much help, he or she analyses the job correctly about half the time. Progress in synthesis can be recorded by noting some mark or grade under the three criteria mentioned above.

The actual extent of record-keeping involved in such a system will depend on many factors, ranging from the teacher's attitude to record-keeping to the styles of work favoured — oral work, for instance can obviously provide good evidence of progress in skills, but would be harder to keep track of, and call for much more snap judgements, than written work. It is possible, however, to make profiles of children's progress however sketchy using this system, and to base judgements about planning further work in skills based on those profiles.

Evaluating Progress in Concept Development

When Peter and Jeanne answered their questions on castles, the teacher wanted them to learn something about castles, as well as foster a couple of skills. What was it he wanted them to learn, and does the slight evidence we have indicate that they learned it?

The best way to approach this question is to analyse what we understand ourselves about castles, about the concept 'castle', and this is most conveniently done by thinking, as it were from the bottom up, in stages, from the simplest, concrete ideas to the complex, abstract ideas, in some such way as this:

(1) Castles are buildings.
(2) Castles are big massive buildings.
(3) Castles were usually built a long time ago.
(4) The purpose of castles was to protect the people inside from armed people outside.
(5) Castles were rationally designed (e.g. with arrow-slits and thick walls) to fulfil this function.
(6) Castles were sited as well as designed, to fulfil this defence function, e.g. on hills.
(7) Castles developed, rationally, under two pressures — (i) increasing wealth, promoting e.g. change from wooden to

masonry castles; and (ii) in response to improvements in means of attack, especially gunpowder weapons.

(8) This development was usually slow, because castles were very expensive items, and major re-building projects represented a major investment.

(9) Ownership or occupation of a castle could confer political status and local influence on a person.

(10) Castles now are often preserved, at some expense, as recreational assets – their function has completely changed.

This is not a definitive breakdown of the concept 'castle'. Someone else might think that you could have a perfectly adequate grasp of the concept 'castle' without knowing item 9, someone else again might want to add items to the list. The analysis is an example of how an idea might be broken down into stages, or steps of a 'ladder', moving from more concrete to more abstract notions, for the purpose of evaluating a child's progress in grasping that idea. Where does Peter stand on the ladder, and what rung could he be encouraged to tackle next? Clearly, he has a firm grasp of stages 1 to 5. There could be a little doubt about his grasp of stage 6, because his answer to question 4 ('Why is the castle on a big mound') is uninformative, and needs expanding before we can be absolutely sure that he grasps the significance of the mound as a site. Suppose we give him the benefit of the doubt on stage 6 – is he ready for the relatively big step to stage, or rung 7, to the idea of castles as developing, changing structures? Fortunately, we have some evidence, a piece written by Peter on the same day, in response to a different sort of task.

> If I was in charge of makeing a castle I wolud pick a high spot dig a trench a round the spot and I wolud billed a big high square shape and knock the corners down and wold builled a round shap on each corner then I wolud make some arrow slits make some square holes and put some canans thir.

This piece disposes of our doubts about Peter's grasp of ladder-stage 6; Peter understands perfectly well about defensive sites. The passage from 'build a big high shape . . . round shape on each corner' illustrates very well that he may either have some understanding of the idea of castles being changed and improved, or he may think that mediaeval builders were extravagant eccentrics who first built square structures and then immediately knocked the corners off. In terms of the 'ladder' metaphor,

Peter is probably reaching out for 'rung' seven, but needs help.

It is, incidentally, very noteworthy that this second exercise has given a clearer view of Peter's understanding of castles, and a clearer indication of what Peter might usefully learn next, than did his answers to the six set questions, a fact which points up the need for a variety of approach.

Exercise 3

On what stage of the 'castle' concept-ladder is Marilyn? (author of the following):

> If I was a man who built castles I wuld build it on a mound so the enemy can-not clime up it and the people that in the castle can get the enemy more easy. And I would put window slits in the wall so men can shoot the arrows at the enemy. And I wuld put a Portcullis so that if the drawbridge was drock down the portcullis would come down.

Abstract concepts lend themselves to the same process of dividing into stages or 'ladders', with the extra difficulty of finding the *concrete* understanding which forms the foot of the ladder, as it were. An illustration would be 'authority', which might 'ladder' as follows:

(1) When somebody tells you what to do and you have to do it.
(2) Different people can tell you different things (e.g. policemen can't keep you in at playtime, teachers can't tell you what time to go to bed).
(3) These differences can be rationally accounted for.
(4) Anybody can confer authority (e.g. our class can vote that Tony will be captain of the football team).
(5) Authority can be taken away from people (e.g. the teacher can stop me being pencils-monitor).
(6) All authority is itself subject to some sort of limits or controls (e.g. teachers can keep you in at home-time, but not forever).
(7) People have to co-operate with authority to make it work.
(8) The powers of an authority can be disputed, reduced or extended because −.
(9) All authority (except the 'authority' of bullies or kidnappers or the like) derives from some theory or belief about the good of the group as a whole.

As with the 'castle' ladder, 'authority' ladders different in emphasis or detail from this one could quite reasonably be drawn up but some ladder like this is necessary to evaluate clearly how much of the concept of 'authority' is understood by the children in this discussion which follows (the contributions are numbered for ease of reference):

(1) Teacher: Who makes the decisions in the classroom?
(2) Andrew: The teacher.
(3) Brenda: Yes.
(4) Teacher: Who makes decisions in the school?
(5) Martin: The caretaker and the headmistress.
(6) Brenda: Sometimes the teacher.
(7) Teacher: Who decides the games you play at playtime?
(8) Martin: The children.
(9) Teacher: How?
(10) Martin: Say one person like me might ask the others if they want to play at football. If they say no I'd keep asking till they said yes to another game.
(11) Andrew: Till we all wanted to play that game.
(12) Brenda: And see what other people want to do.
(13) Teacher: How did you take that decision?
(14) Brenda: Sorting things out.
(15) Teacher: Any other ways?
        (pause)
(16) Teacher: So you are talking. Are there any other ways?
        (pause)
(17) Andrew: Take it in turns.
(18) Martin: You could count and see how many people wanted that game and how many wanted another.
(19) Teacher: Good. What do we call that?
(20) Martin: Vote.
(21) Teacher: Good.

Nobody uses the actual word 'authority' in this little exchange, and indeed one of the interesting and problematic decisions when dealing with an abstract idea which is expressed in a word not usually thought of as suitable 'junior' vocabulary, is the question of at what stage to introduce the word itself. On the whole, the best rule is 'the sooner the better', as children are much less nervous of 'hard words' than adults sometimes think, and also it saves circumlocution and, sometimes, confusion. (For estion 'How many brothers and sisters have you got?' can be quite confusing and the use of the 'hard word' 'sibling' in such a case would actually allow for a much clearer question, once the fairly easy idea of 'sibling' had been acquired.)

Despite the lack of use of the actual word 'authority', however, we can see that Martin and Brenda (at discussion points 5 and 6) have an idea that different sorts of authority exist ('ladder-rung 2). Whether they could go into stage 3, and tell us something about their differences, we cannot tell, because 'Teacher' then takes the group into stage 4, intent on driving towards the idea of authority conferred by 'vote'. In fact the children seem to be pushed a bit towards producing the idea 'vote' when in fact they are dealing (in points 7 to 17) with the more difficult idea of consensus, but the main point is that in retrospect, we might see that if 'Teacher' had had a slightly clearer idea of some sort of conceptual ladder related to the idea of authority, he could either have pursued the head-mistress/caretaker/teacher question, i.e. explored 'ladder-rungs' 2 and 3, or alternatively made a more thorough exploration of 'rung 4', of authority conferred by popular choice. This more thorough explanation of 'rung 4' might have involved discussion of how a team-leader of some kind might be chosen, rather than the trickier area of how a group of children finish up playing cowboys or tig. Only very careful observation of a group would show how the cowboys versus tig question is actually resolved by real children and that observation would reveal a very complicated, shifting process, as the children try to explain, not very successfully, in points 10 to 14.

This whole exchange, brief as it is, illustrates three points of great importance:

(i) Quite young children can usefully discuss abstract concepts.
(ii) This discussion can be perfectly useful and revealing even if the central concept word (e.g. 'authority') is not used.
(iii) The key both to success and to the teacher's ability to evaluate the success, is the teacher's ability to do quite a refined analysis of the concept, through making a 'ladder', or some similar device, before embarking on work involving the concept.

Exercise 4

Make 'concept-ladders' for the following ideas: supermarket, money, law, empire, agriculture, trade, slave, factory.

Exercise 5

In the case of the concept 'empire' can you place Eric and Maitland, on the evidence of the following exchange, somewhere on your 'ladder'?

Teacher:	What's an empire?
Eric:	A big place.
Teacher:	Anything else about it . . .
Eric:	Like a tomb?
Teacher:	Er — well suppose Egypt itself was a big place, would you say that was an empire?
Eric:	No.
Teacher:	What do you have to do to get an empire?
Maitland:	Conquer some place else. It's when you conquer someplace else which isn't where . . . if the Egyptian got, er, somewhere — that's an empire.
Eric:	They could hide in it. Make prisons.
Maitland:	Then they would kill all the people, most of the people and make them slaves.

Exercise 6

Can you place Mary somewhere on your 'trade' ladder, in the light of this piece of her writing?

First the indians lived there and had the furs then some french peple came and they fought at first then they traderd. They traded furs for exchange for guns and things then after a long time they stopped tradeing and peple would buy the furs for money and not trade any more.

Evaluating the Learning of Information

On the face of it, this area of evaluation presents very few problems — someone either knows the Prime Minister's name, or doesn't, and finding out whether they do or not is a straightforward job. The real problem with evaluating children's learning of information is deciding what information children ought to learn, and that in turn is very closely bound up with the matter of analysing and 'laddering' concepts.

The discussion about the concept of authority on pages 142-4 is set in terms of the authority of teachers and of school children — it could equally well consider the authority of policemen, real or fictional kings and princes, or Red Indian chiefs – whatever the subject matter, the understanding the children possessed of the concept 'authority' could have been revealed and enhanced by a well led discussion. Yet if a child was operating at any level of the 'authority' ladder above the most rudimentary, we would expect, if we asked 'Who can tell you what to do?' to get some answer like 'Teachers, policeman, mam and dad'. In other words, possession of some pieces of simple information can be legitimately expected as evidence of understanding of a concept.

You can, of course, understand, say the concept of slavery, in theory, without being able to name any society where slavery existed. Equally, you could be able to recall that 'America had slaves until 1865', without understanding at all well what a slave might be. In practice, however, it would be odd if a child understood what a supermarket was, and yet could not name a local example. Similarly, it would be reasonable to ask a child to name a couple of Red Indian tribes to show that, in that setting, he knows what a 'tribe' is.

Exercise 7

In connection with the concepts listed in Exercise 4, what two or three items of basic factual information would it be reasonable to expect children to learn?

Setting up Tests of Understanding and Progress of Concepts

So far, all our analysis of children's understanding of concepts has been, as it were, static. We have been able to move from saying 'John seems to understand a bit about the idea of "authority" ' to something like 'John's at about stage four on my "authority" ladder', but what we cannot yet say is that John has moved up the ladder since last week or not. To be able to know the answer to that, the crucial question, we must know what stage he was at before we set out to improve his understanding through written work, discussion or whatever.

There are two main problems about this. We do not want to be, or seem to be, eternally giving tests. Secondly, we have to work out exactly what we need to ask the children in the preliminary questioning (or 'pre-test', to use an ugly and offputting, but useful, shorthand): Clearly it would have been inappropriate to ask Andrew, Martin and Brenda (page 143) to define 'authority'. So what do we ask and how do we use the results?

The teacher of Freda, Steven and Jonathan is trying to foster an idea not readily expressed in a single word, namely that there is a crucial difference between societies where everybody has to work at hunting or farming, and societies where there is a sufficiently organised agriculture for a lot of people to be released for great public works, wars of conquest and the like. If we prefer to think of a single word concept to cover this idea, we might say that it represents a fairly early rung in a 'ladder' of the concept 'civilisation'.

The subject-matter is ancient Egypt and the teacher's first move, after looking at some pictures of pyramids and discussion of their huge size, was to get the whole class to write down the answer to this question: 'What would the people need, to build a pyramid?' The children's responses were then briefly discussed and then the teacher launched into a discussion session with the class in which he tried to convey the main idea of the need for a labour-surplus and the role of a good, prosperous agriculture in providing such a surplus. Finally, he asked the class if they would like to add to their lists of things needed for building a pyramid. Below are the responses of three of the children.

A. Freda (List before discussion, or 'pre-test')
   The peaple wold need tools a lot of time to think about how to bilud it and also a lot of time to bilud it they wold need tools, stown, wood, clay, sand, rope.
   (Additions after discussion)
   men. The men how disided to bilud a pyramid have to have a very long time to Do it in the egpture could bilud this pyramid Because when they were working on the farm they have a good skills and they cold hunt there own food.

B. Steven (List before discussion)
   They would need a great lot of time and they would have matearials like – stone, clay, wood, sand, metal, rope.
   (Additions after discussion)
   Water, malet, tools. The Egyptians would need a lot of time because they would have to have food and that would mean they would have to work on the farm. So they had a problem.

C. Jonathan (List before discussion)
   needed – Wood, Rope, stone, water, tools, mallet, kind of chistel mortar wedges paint.
   (Additions after discussion)
   clay picks plans long rods. They would have to have time and enough food and money to keep going in this world.

If we take Jonathan first, it seems that his interest is in the technical problem of pyramid-building ('Kind of chistel . . . wedges' in the first list) and that he has possibly spent the discussion period thinking about the technical rather than the social problem — 'plans' and 'long rods' are interesting technical items on his second list, but his observation about 'time and money' is perfunctory, and in fact one of the points laboured by the teacher in the discussion was that a simple peasant society cannot simply pay some unspecified 'somebody' to build its pyramids for it.

Both Steven and Freda, before any discussion, list 'time' as one of the 'things needed' in pyramid building and so seem ready before the discussion proper, to entertain the idea of problems beyond the merely technical. After the discussion Freda's addition of 'men' to her original list, and the idea that '. . . the Egyptians could build this pyramid because when they were working on the farm they have good skills' could reasonably be taken as a sign of progress towards the key connection between skilful, prosperous agriculture and pyramid building. Steven's second list states the Egyptians' problem of finding surplus labour with great economy, though he seems either not to understand, or not to be impressed by, the solution of conducting agriculture with greater skill.

In summary — Jonathan has been thinking, but not about the question the teacher wanted him to think about, Freda and Steven seem to have made definite progress on the lines the teacher wants, but neither of them have actually clearly stated that better agriculture would create spare labour; they both seem rather hung up on the issue of the time involved in building pyramids. For all three of them it would be reasonable to conclude that it would be unsafe to go on without reinforcing the idea of more efficient agriculture leading to the possibility of labour surplus, perhaps through some work in which the required agricultural surpluses and surplus labour are actually quantified. One great merit of this procedure is that these are much firmer and more useful conclusions about the progress made, and the best way forward, than the teacher was able to make on the informal basis of the childrens' oral work alone: nods of agreement, smiles, a general air of eagerness and interest all contributed to making the teacher in this instance overestimate the childrens' understanding of the key idea. The great merit of written responses to carefully planned questions is precisely this, that it takes us beyond the complacencies of 'I think they got hold of that idea all right' which can very easily be engendered by a few good oral responses and a general buzz of interest and enthusiasm in a classroom. The second major virtue of this particular sequence is that at no point was there a test atmosphere. The children saw the 'pre-test' question as a problem to work at, not a test, as there was no overt element of recall of previous learning, nor was the word 'test' used at any point. The class saw the 'post-test', the invitation to add to their original lists, as a sort of generous concession, a chance to polish up their original work before giving it in, not as any kind of test or check.

Thirdly, the whole thing had the merit of fitting very naturally into the flow of activity, the write-talk-write sequence was quite sensible in itself, and one to which the children were quite accustomed.

The main drawback of this way of testing progress is the premium it puts on writing ability. Clive's work looked like this:

(List before discussion)
   stosne
   tols
   tems
(Additions after discussion)
   md
   tim oft to to do tewrok

The third item in the first list means 'teams' (of workers), which is a pretty reasonable idea to go with stones and tools. 'Tim oft to to do tewrok' means 'Time off to do the work'. This is an analysis of the central problem of the need for spare labour which is nearly as good as Freda's or Steven's, and better than Jonathan's. In its original form, however, it was virtually illegible and the teacher had to ask Clive what it meant, having first had to resist the strong and easily formed impression that it did not mean much, and that Clive's poor literacy faithfully reflected poor understanding.

Jonathan's work, on the other hand, looked neat and legible, spelling was reasonable, and the first impression was misleadingly favourable.

Once we are dealing with groups of more than four or five children, written work in some form, which we can analyse at leisure (or good quality tape recording of oral work) is normally the only reliable tool for evaluating progress. But good writing can flatter shallow content, just as poor writing can disguise thoughtfulness and we have to watch out for both traps and be prepared to talk to individuals when we really can't grasp what they are trying to communicate by writing. A good rule to follow is that any task set as a test should also be a worthwhile task in itself, and set in an appropriate medium. The section on 'Levels of Difficulty' suggests ways of making tasks both generally easier or harder and also, specifically, ways of setting work for children of very limited literacy, e.g. through drawing. All the advice there applies equally to tasks designed as pre-tests or evaluative tasks.

Exercise 8

Try to devise simple 'pre-tests' to test understanding either of the concepts you worked on in Exercise 4 (page 144) or any concept of your choice, short work-sequences to follow the pre-tests, and 'post-tests' to show up advances in understanding the concept.

What to Do with the Results of Pre-tests and Post-tests

Being able to talk with some modest degree of precision about childrens' conceptual progress and progress in skills, in the "topic" area gives us a great general benefit. It is obviously good for teachers to be able to refine their perception about Jonathan's topic work, and make clearer distinctions between Jonathan's areas of strengths and weaknesses and those of Freda, both in order to communicate usefully with other teachers, and with parents, and in order to sort out their own long-term planning for topic work. Perhaps even more important is the guidance that good analysis of childrens' state of understanding, and progress, can give in the day-to-day planning of a topic.

Sometimes this guidance is very clear. If, for example, children are very hesitant about interpreting pictures then clearly they will have to be taught and encouraged in the skill of interpreting pictures before we can go on to the more ambitious interpreting, evaluating, extrapolating picture-work that we had originally planned. Similarly, if we ask children to 'Write *one* good thing and *one* bad thing, about living in a Stone Age cave', and we get a lot of answers like these:

Good	Bad things
Safety	Dark
Warm if faceing right way	Cold if faceing cold wind
Do not have to work at	Might be wet
biulding it	Animals might live there
	Cant change how it is

In such a case we might be well advised to, say, go straight to the full-scale comparison of stone-age and modern life-styles which originally we were not going to attempt for another two or three weeks, because evaluation through comparison is clearly an easier task for these children than we assumed in our early planning.

This result, incidentally, of the preliminary work showing that the children know and understand more than we gave them credit for, is a very common one, in our experience, with junior-age children. (It is obviously also a more difficult result to cope with, as it might involve permanently ditching a whole phase of our planned work, than a result showing children to be less knowledgeable or skilful than we thought, which may only involve postponement of planned work.)

Where concepts rather than skills are principally involved, working out how to react to test results can be more difficult.

In the case of Freda, Steven, Jonathan and Clive working on ancient Egypt, we can say two important things:

(i) None of them yet clearly grasp the idea of agricultural surplus providing surplus labour – so we cannot yet safely move on to questions like 'What else could the Egyptians do with their extra men?' (e.g. wars of conquest). We have to consolidate.

(ii) None of the three, not even Jonathan, is so at sea with the idea that we have to go right back to some much simpler idea, e.g. that food has to be grown and does not just materialise in shops.

In other words, as well as showing up interesting and possibly useful facts about individuals, such as Jonathan's technological bent and Clive's literacy problems, the tests show that we are probably planning and working at about the right level.

This next result leads to a different possible conclusion. Pre-test question: 'What animals might you find on a farm?' Alan's response: 'dog cat budigy.' Work then followed on pictures of farm animals and farm machinery, followed by oral discussion of different types of farm. Post-test question: 'What animals and other things might you find on a farm?' Alan's response: dogs, ahen, car, curtins.

What Alan takes farm to mean is farm-*house* – hence his second list, which is of creatures and things to be seen in the picture in the immediate vicinity of the farm-house. He needs to learn what the concept 'farm' entails, before he can move on to the teacher's intended goal of establishing that there are different kinds of farm – arable, dairy, mixed, etc. In other words, Alan is not stupid, its simply that we have started a rung or two too high up this particular concept ladder for him.

Sometimes a result can make us doubt whether we are on the right 'ladder' at all, like this one:

The teacher wanted to establish the idea that water transport, in the pre-industrial era, was normally easier than land transport, and asked by way of pre-test the simple question: 'Would it be easier in those days (the middle ages) to move a big block of stone by road or by boat?' The one-word responses from the group split roughly 50-50 between road and boat. The work done next concentrated on the physical short-comings of medieval roads and the greater ease of movement through water, in terms of mud, ruts and the like. The post-test question was 'Now say *with reasons* which way you would have moved the block.' Joan's response was: 'Water way because you would not have all the horses just one boat and a pole so it would be cheap. On road you would be very slow.' Simon's response was: 'On rivers because the road was all mud and it would take ages to drag it and on a river boat it could just sail along.'

Joan has evidently started to climb some concept-ladder which we might describe as 'economics' or, alternatively expressed, she is a lot farther up the ladder of the concept of 'transport' than the teacher allowed for. In this case it would be necessary to try out Joan's response on Simon and the rest of the group and see if they respond to and grasp this higher level of approach to the problem. It may well have been that the very concrete terms of the test and the work have encour-aged responses more concrete, at a lower level, than the children are capable of.

Exercise 9
Do the following pre-test, post-test results indicate that the teacher has pitched the work too high, too low, or about right? Has progress been made between pre-test and post-test?

Example A Topic on 'weather'. Teachers goal — to establish that weather phenomena have serious economic effects, as well as merely inconveniencing people.
Pre-test 'Who might be glad if it rained in the summer?'
Richard's response: gardenrs, farmers if it had had been dry a lot ranecoat sellers.
Post-test 'Who might be sorry if it rained in the summer?'
Richard's response: ice cream men road digers children.
Example B Topic on 'television'. Teacher's goal — to establish the economic reasons for TV advertising.

Pre-test 'Why do you think they have adverts on ITV?'
Carol's response: Som of them are nice i lik the cat advetrs.
Post-test 'What would happen if they had no adverts on ITV?'
Carol's response: Peple would not wacth them.
Example C Topic on 'ancient Egypt'. Teacher's goal – understanding of mechanics of an irrigation system.
Pre-test 'How might they get the water from the Nile onto the fields?
John's response: They wold all have to agree how to do it and which field wold have it first and who wold carry the buckets with it in in turns. They wold use buckets.
Post-test 'How did "irrigation" work'
John's response: They dig canals and smaller canals coming off the canals and had shadufs and wheels to get the water up.
Example D Topic on 'Normans'. Teacher's goal – develop concept of 'conquer'.
Pre-test 'What does it mean to conquer somewhere?'
Adrian's response: If they come and kill most peple and kill them and make them do things.
Post-test 'Now we've learned how the Normans conquered England – how might they have conquered Scotland?'
Adrian's response: Has a battle first and win and kill the King and some peple bild castles get peple to do new laws and get peple on ther side so some peple mought like them.

Notes on Exercises

Exercise 1

Jeanne's answers are brief, sometimes too brief, (as in number 3) for us to be able to tell if she has understood, so something like 'Good. I like number 6 where you tell me a lot. Try to tell me more about the narrow slits in number 3'. (Spelling – 'clime' in number 4 should be corrected.)

Exercise 2

(Lester) 'castle' and/or 'stones' ought to be corrected. Thing to praise is his good habit of explaining phenomena very succinctly.

(Julie) should be praised for fluency and asked to tell us more about why the hill is 'the best place'.

(John) 'many' and/or 'there' should be corrected. The 'sentence' to praise is probably the second one, ('The castle is good . . .') which is quite long and complex. John can be praised for getting several ideas fairly successfully into one 'sentence', and encouraged to finish off that particular sentence properly by some phrase like 'we had to go home'.

Exercise 3

Marilyn seems to be pretty securely on rung 5 and probably would have no difficulty with rung 6. She shows no sign in this particular piece of reaching out for rung 7.

Exercise 4

The construction of concept ladders depends on the teachers own interpretation of a concept, so there are no right answers here. Be sure, however, that your ladders go up high enough, as junior teachers are in more danger of underestimating, than of overestimating, what their children can do. Thus, the 'supermarket' ladder ought to extend up to the idea of the controversy about whether supermarkets are somehow socially less desirable than corner shops, 'money' ought to stretch up to encompass the idea of credit, and of 'the price of money', i.e. interest rates and so on. It is much better to have a ladder whose top rungs your children never reach (at least in junior school), than one which stops too short for the ablest children.

Exercise 5

Whatever your ladder on 'empire' is like, Eric must be regarded as having hardly begun to scale it. Maitland's idea of empire is unsophisticated but clearly includes the primary idea that it is 'somewhere else that you conquer'.

Exercise 6

The last five words may show that Mary is using the word 'trade' with no understanding at all of its meaning — likelier, though, is that she simply equates 'trade' with 'barter'.

Exercise 9

Example A. Richard shows he has the rudiments of the idea in the pre-test, but the post-test does not seem to show any advance. It may be that he has not learned anything between the two tests, or that the post-test itself is too simple in form to draw out what he knows. Perhaps something more taxing as a pre-test, for instance 'Is there any kind of weather that nobody can gain money from? would have been more revealing.

Example B. Carol seems to show no idea at all of the economic dimension of advertising in her pre-test answer – the post-test response has the merit of being incontrovertibly true. Obviously Carol needs first to understand that advertisements are designed, and carefully designed, to sell things to people before she can take the next complicated step and understand that advertisers might pay other people, like television firms, to show their advertisements. And before that, of course, she must also understand that TV is a business, that one way or another, people do not beam pictures at her just for fun.

Example C. John's pre-test response is interesting about the social and political arrangements needed to make irrigation systems work. The teacher is aiming too low in concentrating on the mechanics of irrigating. The post-test shows a fair grasp of the mechanics, but one way or another the more interesting ideas present in the pre-test response have vanished. John's intellectual movement, on the strength of the two scraps of evidence before us, has been backwards, away from the abstract, towards the concrete.

Example D. The pre-test response contains the germ of the idea of conquest, and the post-test shows Adrian developing it quite well, especially in the phrase 'get people on their side so some people might like them'.

10 OBJECTIVES AND PLANNING

The way a teacher plans work on a topic obviously makes a great potential difference both to the success of the childrens' learning and to the
success with which that learning can be evaluated. But what constitutes
a 'good' or 'bad' plan? Two examples might be illuminating.

Outline Plan A – Topic on 'Shops'

(i) Introduce topic by discussion of various types of shop in Briarfield
shopping centre. List different types.
(ii) Visit Briarfield centre.
(iii) Make notes of information collected on Briarfield visit. Children to
draw shop of own choice for frieze.
(iv) Move on to shops that are not 'shops' – garages, hairdressers,
swimming pools.
(v) Move on to shops in other countries – bazaars etc., use pictures.

Outline Plan B – Topic on 'Shops'

(i) Children classify shops on Briarfield. Discuss classifications and lists.
(ii) Visit Briarfield. Children count numbers of people coming out of
different shops in ten-minute period.
(iii) Make block-graph of information gathered under (ii); make frieze;
use words 'turnover' and 'profit'.
(iv) Children discuss whether following are 'shops' – garage, hairdresser,
swimming pool.
(v) Pictures of bazaars etc. – put questions like 'is this a shop?'
Guided reading on shops in other countries.

Neither of these is a masterpiece of educational planning, but Plan B
offers four crucial advantages.

First, it is somewhat clearer than A about what the children will do.
It is clear, for example in item (i) that the children, not the teacher, will
do the listing and classifying, and in (iv) and (v) it is made much clearer
what the children will be doing in Plan B than in the unhelpful formula
of 'move on to' of Plan A.

Secondly, it is easier to guess from Plan B what some of the educational purposes of the exercise might be. B is clearly interested in the
concept 'shop' and in the idea of 'turnover' and 'profit'. In item (iv), A

suggests an interest also in exploring the limits of the concept 'shop',
but not very clearly.

Thirdly, it is vastly easier to work out from Plan B how the success
of the topic might be evaluated: children using more complicated
definitions of 'shop', and correct use of the terms 'turnover' and 'profit'
can all be evaluated with a moderate degree of precision.

Fourthly, and perhaps most importantly, it is easier to ask pertinent
questions or suggest improvements to Plan B than to Plan A. For
instance, if use of the terms 'turnover' and 'profit' are wanted, would
using a story containing the words be a good idea? Could these children
actually show the relationships: big turnover – small profit, small turnover – large profit in some simple visual form? Is ten minutes really
long enough to get the point that many more people come out of the
supermarket than out of the shoe-shop? What if nobody comes out of
the shoe-shop? As to the concept 'shop' itself – what if someone very
early on says 'a garage is a sort of shop, isn't it? – what, in other words,
is their understanding of 'shop' before we start?

Because Plan B, although only a dozen words longer than A, is so
much more informative, we can be quite sharp and constructive about
it. With Plan A we would first have to ask very basic questions like
'Who lists the types of shop?', 'Why are we visiting Briarfield?', 'What
"information" are we gathering?', 'What does "move on to . . ." mean?'.

In the late fifties and sixties a movement began designed to help
teachers to plan their work better by the four criteria we have just
suggested and illustrated, i.e. that teachers should think in terms of
what the children will do, not in terms of what teachers will 'introduce'
or 'move on to', that what the children will *learn* from the activity
should be made very clear; that attention would be paid right from the
start to how that learning might be evaluated; and finally that the
planning should be of such precision that pitfalls and difficulties can be
foreseen and avoided before the work actually starts. This movement,
which was known as the 'objectives' or 'behavioural objectives'
movement, has been both extremely valuable and given rise to a lot of
misunderstanding, confusion and some hostility.

Behavioural Objectives

A 'behavioural' objective tells you precisely what a child will be able to
do at the end of a learning process, e.g. when asked the date of the
battle of the Little Bighorn, the child will respond '1876'. We can

certainly make very precise plans on the basis of such objectives.

'The children will learn the names and dates of the three following battles between Plains Indians and whites . . . after five minutes the children will be asked the date of the Little Bighorn battle'. The trouble with objectives at this level of precision in topic work is obvious — they seem to apply readily only to the learning of information, and not to lend themselves to the development of concepts and skills. If we asked the children, for instance, 'Were the Plains Indians nomads?' we might specify that the children would answer 'Yes' — but we would want more than that from them if we were to be satisfied that they had understood the concept 'nomad' and at what level they had understood it, and exactly what we would get from them would be very difficult or impossible to say in advance. 'Yes, they went about on horses', as a response, might represent a successful advance up the 'ladder' of the idea of nomadism for one child, but an actual regression for another.

The difficulty and evident inappropriateness of behavioural objectives in the setting of topic work has had unfortunate effects. Some people have rejected the idea entirely, and settled for the old string-of-ideas type of planning, like that in Plan A for the topic on 'shops'. Others think it inappropriate to be as specific even as Plan A, and would leave it to the inspiration of the moment to decide how a topic will progress. Perhaps the worst of all choices is to adopt the language of objectives, and with it a spurious air of precision, without the substance: hence 'objectives' like 'To give an idea of the life of the Plains Indians', or 'To bring the children to a sympathetic understanding of Plains Indian life'.

The essential thing to hang onto is the need for a way of planning that answers the three basic questions 'What are the children going to do? What are they going to learn? How will I know they have learned it?' If we combine the idea of objectives with our idea of concept-ladders and skills progression, outlined in the previous section, and look again at the topic of 'shops' we might come up with a formula something like this.

Objectives (i) Concepts

>   Concept of a 'shop',
>   concept of 'profit',
>   concept of 'turnover',

Objectives (ii) Skills

>   Classifying

interpreting;
translating;

will be the skills most emphasised.

Now this little set of objectives is, of course, a shorthand, but a very convenient one. 'Concept of a "shop" ' presented as an objective is shorthand for something like 'I think the class are generally on level one of the "shop" ladder, that is, they conceive of shops as being butchers', bakers', etc. I want to push them up to level two, when they will understand that anywhere where goods are exchanged for money might be seen as a shop and, if possible, up to level three, where they understand that there are marginal cases, like garages, which we do not call 'shops', but which it would not be silly to call shops, because they have many of the characteristics of shops.'

'Concept-objectives', in fact, always imply, obviously that the teacher knows roughly where the children stand on some concept ladder, or is going to carry out a pre-test to find out, and is going to help the children up one or more rungs.

Similarly, skills objectives like 'classifying' must mean that the teacher plans to take steps to improve the children's power of classification, from whatever (known) stage they are at now, up to some specified higher stage of expertise.

This way of looking at objectives falls a good way short of the precision of fully behavioural objectives, but it does ensure that the planning based on them will contain clear answers to two of our three basic questions – 'What will the children learn, and how will I know they've learned it?' The answer to the other question, 'What will the children do?' is bound up with the teacher's ingenuity and local resources, the children's experience and enthusiasms and so on, but the answers to that question also will be referred back all the time to the objectives – if we think it a good idea to have a little play about dissatisfied customers complaining to a shopkeeper, we must ask, why? Is it developing the concept of 'shop' or 'profit' or what? Or is it developing some other important concept which we overlooked in our initial planning and, if so, what? Or is it just passing the time?

Selecting Objectives

One thing will have struck any teacher about the two little topic-plans on shops, namely that the emphasis of the plans could quite reasonably have been very different. We could have stressed the nature of shops as being, as it were, machines for selling things, leading to consideration of advertising, and of questions like how shopkeepers know how much to charge, why prices sometimes vary from week to week, how shop-keepers know how much cat-food to buy in, and why they sell brand x and not brand z. We could, alternatively, have looked on the shop as basically a work-place, and learned about how shops are managed, how they are owned, what work shop-assistants do and how they learn to do it. No doubt you can think of other approaches as well.

Whichever emphasis we chose, some concepts like 'profit' and 'shop' itself, would probably appear in any set of objectives, but at other points, we would have to choose between lists of concepts like, say, 'advertising, shop, profit, price, rent, retail, wholesale, market' and 'shop, profit, manager, chain-store, supermarket, wages, training'. Put more pretentiously, but accurately, we would have to choose between a purely economic approach, and a mixed economic/sociological approach.

We could try to cover all important aspects of shops in one single ambitious topic, but this would be very difficult to manage. One apparently minor concept connected with shops is 'change' (as in 'change from a pound'). One young teacher, checking on her class of 7-year-olds' understanding of 'change', checking merely as a preliminary to the main work of a topic on shops, found the following range of understandings.

(i) Two children with, it seems, no idea at all of what 'change' was;
(ii) several children who knew that shops give change, but thought the change was an arbitrary sum, not the product of money tendered *minus* price of goods bought;
(iii) the majority group who knew that change was money tendered *minus* price of goods bought;
(iv) one girl who volunteered the information that you have to give the correct fare on one-man buses because otherwise the queue would be held up, and that one-man buses were to save paying wages to a conductor, and so make more profit for 'the bus people'.

Shepherding this class up the rungs of four or five economic concepts, making sure that no-one was either left too far behind or bored by being too far ahead was taxing and time-consuming, and the teacher concluded that only one major aspect of shops could be covered unless the class were to spend a whole term on 'shops', at the grave risk of boredom.

So, in general terms, how do we choose our approach? At one level, this is a philosophical question. We might have decided, for instance, that we will run six major topics per year, that three of them will be principally devoted to natural science matters and three to social sciences. Of our three social science topics, we decided that this year one will have a historical, change-in-time, slant, and we have decided to do the Normans; we want one of the others to deal with a present-day social institution and we have chosen 'Work' as a topic, and our third, we have decided, should deal with some aspect of economics. 'Shops' fits that slot, so 'shops' gets an economic emphasis, not by our arbitrary choice, but as part of a rational scheme, aiming at some sort of conceptual balance, however crude.

For most people, however, the real problems of selecting objectives begin at this point. Suppose we have decided that we want to deal with a present-day social institution, and it strikes us that the law is a very important institution, and that by studying it we might kill two birds with one stone and teach children a little about how laws have changed over time, and might change again. So we have a blank piece of paper, headed 'topic on law'. How do we decide on a reasonably small number of concepts, to constitute our concept-objectives?

One useful approach is simply to write yourself a fairly short paragraph, at adult level, stating what you see to be the interest of the topic, and then underline the important, difficult ideas which occur in the paragraph. You might get a paragraph like this on 'Law'.

Laws are different from rules, say the rules of a school, or of football, because everyone has to keep them. Yet they change – a whole new lot of laws has had to be made since the invention of cars, for instance. Also laws change when people's attitudes change – we no longer hang thieves, for instance. There are a lot of people involved in running the law, with different roles – policemen, lawyers, judges, juries and there are a lot of laws that have nothing much to do with punishment and crime at all – such as laws about buying and selling houses – civil law as it is called.

We can now make up our objectives list as follows: Law and rule, are obvious candidates. It would, however, not be very informative to put down made |and change as objectives, but the idea behind the underlining of those two apparently innocuous words is a vital one – that law does not descend from the sky, but gets invented by people to meet situations. The best way to express this idea might be as a sentence, such as *Laws are made and changed for reasons* rather than as a single-word concept. *Attitude, role, lawyer, judge, jury, crime* and *civil law* are pretty clear-cut targets — *policeman* is underlined and included not because it is an obviously difficult concept, but because observation suggests that many junior children think that policemen make laws and decide punishments, in other words, the idea of a policeman's role is more difficult to children than might appear.

The list now has eleven items, and experience suggests that this is the outside limit for a useful preliminary-planning list of concept objectives, if only because the progress of the topic, the revelation of children's understanding and the divergence of children's interests will throw up other worthwhile concepts which you may decide ought to be attacked. The topic could be one minute old when someone asks 'Miss, what's 'prosecute' mean?' or the work on making up new laws for a society that has developed space travel may be so absorbing and useful leading into, say, the problems of the justice of forbidding ten people to do something which will inconvenience five other people, that you abandon objectives which you think less important.

With all its potential limitations, though, the list is at least a decent starting point for planning, and by starting from adult preoccupations avoids the cardinal sin of triviality. Starting from what one imagines to be children's preoccupations can all too easily lead to a planned programme confined to panda-cars, police-dogs, writing exciting stories about robberies, and the like. There is nothing wrong with police-dogs; as a starting-point for learning about police powers, they are very useful and interesting, but somewhere along the way we ought to ask what happens if the dog bites someone who later turns out to be innocent. Such a question is much more likely to be put, and thought about, if our mental agenda contains apparently 'adult' items like 'Police-powers of. Complaints procedure', rather than simply 'Visit of police-dog and handler — Tuesday', and unless such questions are put, a good time may be had by all, but conceptual development will only take place, if at all, by chance.

Skills-objectives can be more nearly left to look after themselves since there are after all only a limited number of intellectual skills, and reasonably varied and imaginative planning of activities will usually see to it that all the skills get used over a period of a week or two. However, it is worth checking that this is so, and asking yourself whether the children are being required by your scheme to, say, extrapolate at all, and if they are not, trying to devise a worthwhile extrapolation exercise of some kind at some point. It is also worth checking that the first few hours of the work on the topic do not involve too many uses of the same intellectual skill, interest is generated or lost largely at the start of topics, so the more variety of activity at the start the better.

'Key Concepts'

An alternative, or complementary way of arriving at a set of concept-objectives is referred to on pp. 19-22 in the 'Context' section, and involves the use of 'key' concepts as guidelines. This might work particularly well where the topic chosen fits fairly clearly under some discipline or subject heading. 'Normans' in our three-topic scheme would be a good case – we may in the course of doing the topic use all manner of materials and ideas drawn from all sorts of areas, from maths to art, but basically this is an historical topic. As an historical topic, we may find it helpful to organise our thinking under a few main headings, or 'key' ideas, ideas which would be relevant to any historical topic, by reason of the nature of history itself as an area of study – that is ideas like power, change and continuity, ideology, culture.

Tactically it is sometimes more useful to think in terms of 'key questions' rather than key concepts, arriving at our concept-list in this way:

Q.   What CHANGES were going on at this time?
A.   Well, the big change was that a new group of rulers the Normans, *took over* England.
Q.   Who had the POWER in this society?
A.   There was a *hierarchy*, going from the King through a *nobility*, down to the ordinary people, who had very little power.
Q.   What were the leading IDEAS of the time?
A.   The nobles had an ideal called *chivalry*, based on an admiration of military prowess, *Christianity* was a powerful religious force.
Q.   What was distinctive about the CULTURE of the Normans?
A.   The *material culture* was pretty simple, largely based on *peasant agriculture*, though there was some *trade* and urban life. Literacy was not widespread: the *Church* was the focus of the arts and literature.

The italicised words, in the 'answers' to the questions give us a manageable list of ten concept objectives.

We still, of course, have important decisions to make. Do we actually want to deal with the idea of, say, 'Church' as a repository of culture, or would we rather miss it out? We might want to work on the moral questions raised by the Conquest, the rights and wrongs of invasion, or on the ins and outs of castle-building, or on various other legitimate objectives not apparently thrown up by this approach. However, the 'key-concepts' approach will always give us some kind of start on planning, and it will tend to give us a start in the direction of worth-while, non-trivial preoccupations. It is probably particularly useful in areas where we are not expert ourselves.

APPENDIX

ILLUSTRATIVE TOPICS

I   'DESERT ISLAND'

This topic involves the children pretending that they are wrecked on a desert island, where they encounter all kinds of problems.

The reasons for using this topic are:

(1)   It provides lots of opportunities for children to solve problems. These may be technological (designing a trap) or social, arising from the fact that human beings live in groups. The advantage of 'desert island' is that the children can be asked to identify and solve many of the problems human beings have encountered during their long past. Problem-solving takes many forms; it may be of a simple trial and error kind; it may involve in the first instance thinking of a multiplicity of possible answers and then evaluating them; or it may involve making a decision in the light of a number of specific factors. Problems are often best solved when a group of people test their ideas in consultation with each other and reach a consensus. Whatever the method of problem-solving used it may be helpful to children's future learning if they are encouraged to state exactly how they tackled a particular problem. If they can do so, they will make explicit a number of techniques which, given subsequent problems, they can consciously select and use again.

(2)   While 'desert island' can involve the use of books, e.g. to find out what animals, vegetation, etc. there will be in a given part of the world, it need not require any books at all. Children can make use of their own day-to-day experience.

(3)   It can be a means of developing a wide range of concepts: survival, settlement, democracy, justice, treaty, compromise, navigation, communicating, vote, election — to mention only a few.

(4)   It can be a means of teaching understandings about society; e.g. that people live together to help and be helped, for the sake of company and for protection.

(5)   A simulation exercise (as we call this kind of topic) allows the teacher to determine just how simple or complex is the society the children study; twentieth-century industrial society is very complex and not at all easy to understand. 'Desert island' can be just as simple or complex as a given group of children can cope with.

Introductory Activity

At the beginning of a topic the teacher's first concern is to motivate the group. There are various ways of doing this. Here we suggest the teacher uses a story (not more than three minutes long) of how the whole class come to be shipwrecked without any adults. He asks the children what they would need to survive on the island, so introducing the first major concept to be tackled.

Survival

One possible move is to put this word on the board and explain it, but we would suggest that it is better to let the children build it up themselves and only introduce the new concept word when they have established what human beings need to survive. So we ask the class what they need to stay alive on the island. The teacher can hold a discussion with the class listing suggestions on the board or ask the children to write down individually as many things as they can or divide the children into groups of 4 to 6, working together to produce one list. We prefer the last method. Whatever the technique adopted, the teacher should encourage the children to produce not just one idea but several. We call this 'multiple response' and being able to do it is regarded as a sign of creative ability. It can however be deliberately fostered by teachers who make it explicit to the children that is what they want. One further point – it is not desirable to insist that the children write complete sentences when they make their lists, for to do so would be to set a long, laborious task for children with limited literary skills, and children can often think a lot better and faster than they can write.

Here are some examples of what eight- and nine-year-old children suggested:

> Richard produced a list of 29 items beginning: food, nets, matches, cages, flint, wood, string, eggs . . . canoes, traps, sails. He has produced lots of ideas, a point for congratulation, all of them very 'concrete'.

> Karen produced a shorter list but one at a higher level of abstraction: warmth, shelter, protection, 'health aids', date record, means of communication and 'someone experienced if possible'. Her ability

to give a list at a higher level of abstraction probably indicates her more advanced conceptual development.

Barrie, interestingly enough, produced the following list:

(1) Warmth:	(2) Food:	(3) Drink:
dried wood	pineapples	coconut milk
flint	coconuts	juice from pine-
	bananas	apples

He has spontaneously classified his items under 'concrete' but very useful headings.

Human beings acquire at quite a young age the habit of classifying and categorising. Young children may make erroneous classifications and describe all men as Daddy or all animals as dogs. It is well known to educationists that concept-formation involves classification. Young children sort beads into groups and gradually form number concepts. The extent to which older learners classify is often overlooked. Every secondary school essay is in part a classification exercise where the learner, having collected a lot of data from different sources, has to see which items go together and group them under some appropriate label which becomes the subject of a paragraph. In the stage between the infant sorting his beads and the adolescent writing his essay, children need lots of practice in classifying data of all kinds in lots of different ways. It seems probable too that making classifications and labelling groups promotes the development of conceptual understanding. In this group of children then we found children producing responses at a number of different levels. The teacher going round the class can make suggestions to each child appropriate to his work. He therefore congratulates Richard on producing lots of ideas and, with a view to raising the level of abstraction at which he is operating, suggests he groups together those which seems to be of a like kind. Then Richard can be encouraged to suggest labels for them: tools; transport, etc.

Exercise 1

Here is David's list. What evaluation would you make of it? What helpful comments can you make to him? Are any questions appropriate?

    climb trees for food
    burn wood
    blancits from leaves

fight against wild animals
boats if there was any svivers

The next stage is to ask the children to evaluate the suggestions the whole group has produced. Ask them which items on the list they have made are essential and which items would be less essential? Are any of them luxuries? Our particular group of children reduced their lists to water, food, shelter and protection. At this point the teacher introduced and began to use the concept-word survival. The children used it too. They decided that they might be able to survive without food or water for several days in favourable conditions but only for an hour or two, in severe conditions. There was a considerable argument about how important shelter was; one girl made a case that protection was more important than any other single thing. What use was it looking for food or building a shelter if you were under attack? We would emphasise the importance of this discussion, a process which encourages the testing of ideas and thinking aloud. In the final stage the children were asked to make judgements and support their judgements with reasons.

The teacher will appreciate that in this situation there is no single 'right' answer; in fact one understanding which emerged from our discussion was that a great deal might depend on the particular conditions on the island.

It is worth studying the children's lists carefully at this stage because they may suggest a helpful way forward. For example, some of the children have begun spontaneously to generate and solve more problems, e.g. Sharon says 'traps for wild animals' while Karen says the group will need a date record. Comments like these may suggest a series of technological problems to be solved by drawing or model making; de Bono has pointed the way for us here with his dog-exercising machine. The teacher might ask them, say, to devise and draw traps to catch specific animals. They could be provided with a picture of the chosen creature and three or four pieces of data about its habits. Each design should be accompanied by an explanation, oral or written as to how it works. Other possibilities include a trap which will catch an animal without hurting it; a device for keeping snakes out of the house; a way of storing water or carrying water; a way of keeping track of the date or of telling time on the island.

At this stage the teacher's main task is to make sure the children think through their problem in all its stages. Confronted with a question like 'What will we need on the island?' some children will leap to the abstraction 'protection' without considering the ramifications of the

problem. The teacher must ask: 'From what dangers do we need
protection? Do we act differently to protect ourselves from snakes,
hostile natives and bears? Exactly what would we need to do to be
secure? If the children suggest a moat and drawbridge how would they
make a drawbridge?'

Thinking the task through however does not necessarily mean hours
of 'work' cutting up paper and card. It may involve drawings together
with a model drawbridge made of string and balsa wood. The 'date
record' would be made sufficiently thoroughly to establish that the
child had determined the principles of its construction, simplicity,
clarity, provision for recording the passage of days, months and years,
but it would not involve making the record for several months and
years which would be a monotonous and not particularly educative
mechanical exercise.

Exercise 2

The children decide they must invent their own money for use on the
island and a group of children are given the task of designing money.
What would you as a teacher consider the essential features of a successful response to this task? What questions could you ask the group of
children running the 'mint' to enable them to think out the basic
principles which would underlie the design of the money?

An alternative strategy for stimulating the kind of creative ability
shown by inventors might be to take Robert's idea that the shipwrecked party might make weapons from bits of wreckage. The teacher
might introduce a collection of materials as wreckage from the ship
which has washed up on the beach and involve the children to make
models of useful objects out of them. A preliminary discussion of an
example might be helpful before they start. Here are some pieces of
wood with a few nails in it, some cloth, some rope; in the lifeboat there
is a hammer, a saw and one of the girls had a pair of scissors. What useful things could we make? Which of those you have suggested would be
best? This kind of work could be done in miniature within the classroom or something like a shelter could be erected out of doors in fine
weather if the teacher wished. Work of this kind would be brought to a
useful conclusion by asking the inventors to explain their procedures
and to say how their inventions would be used.

There are obviously many themes that could be taken up in this
general 'desert island' setting, but for illustrative purposes, in the next
few pages we suggest how a teacher might go about promoting a few of

the more obviously appropriate concepts.

Teaching the Concept 'Climate'

One way is to provide the children with some data about the island. Since children in the concrete operational stage can cope with four variables, we limit the data to not more than four essential items in the first place. For example:

> It is very hot and sticky during the middle of the day.
> It gets dark at seven o'clock every evening.
> It gets light about six o'clock in the morning.
> It rains heavily every afternoon about four o'clock.

Exercise 3

3.1 Try to devise some questions to develop the understanding that peoples lives are adapted to the climate they live in.

3.2 Choose a different climate, e.g. arctic and make up four short items of data about an island in the arctic area. Then introduce the concept 'environment' and devise some questions to reinforce understanding of adaptation to climate and environment.

Alternatively, if the teachers can lay hands on copies of the *National Geographical* magazine or some other good source of pictorial material he can give the children pictures of their island, its flora and fauna and from this they can try to infer its climate. Is your island hot or cold? Similarly with such pictorial material the teacher can introduce the concept environment. This is where you are going to live – Look at the pictures of the coast, the forests, the animals that live there, the sharks in the sea; these are your environment. Such pictures could be accompanied by appropriate reading materials and when the children have gathered information about their world they could record it in a large composite picture of their island home including all its main and essential features. A task of this kind is not necessarily a purely artistic one, there is a substantial cognitive element too, for instance the children, in discussion, would be led to identify what for instance were the important characteristics of their environment which must be recorded in the picture. In other words the making of the picture would involve them in the application of important conceptual understandings e.g. concepts such as 'importance', 'characteristics', 'environment'. It is desirable that they should add captions to the picture explaining it and using any new words they have learned.

Where the teacher has only limited materials available, he can divide the class into groups and arrange for them to be shipwrecked on different kinds of islands with different vegetation, animal life and climate — they would all encounter the same problems. This could lead to some useful comparisons between different ways of life, and to the formation of important general understandings.

Teaching the Concepts of Site and Settlement

This logically follows the tasks on survival. The teacher says, or a work-card does it for him, 'Where are you going to live?' Here again the teacher provides data. This may be quite simple:

Will you live in a cave?
Will you make a shelter on the beach?
Will you live on the top of the cliff overlooking the beach?

These may need illustrating with pictures. Some children may need help by way of supplementary questions to think this through, e.g.:

Which of these will be safest? (from the sea, the animals, the enemies)
Which will be most convenient?
Which will be the most comfortable in bad weather?
What will be advantages and disadvantages of living in a cave?

For older and more able children a picture map can be introduced.

Exercise 4

4.1 Draw such a picture map of part of the island and put in a hill, fresh water supply, the sea coast with a cave, banana trees, etc. In planning your map build into it one site which has obvious advantages with reference to access to food, water, shelter and defence.

4.2 With such a picture map the danger could be that children will spot the 'right place' straight away and you will have worked quite a long time only to find that you occupy the child in only a few minutes' thought, so add some questions to the picture map, e.g.:

Is the place you have chosen a good place to defend?
Can you easily get to fresh water?
In choosing a place which is more important, nearness to food or water?
Think of some others.

More able children will be able to make a choice between two different sites, each with its own advantages and disadvantages.

Exercise 5

5.1 Try to draw a map where the bright child will have to hesitate between two 'good' places and give reasons for his choice. Another version on the same kind of task is to introduce more variables, e.g. more dangers (native tribesmen), more advantages (land for growing crops), swamps, a safe harbour, etc.
5.2 Take your original map and see if you can make a new version harder in both the ways suggested above.

You could therefore, if you know the levels of ability of children in your class, have a number of desert island tasks which suit them individually. Finally it is desirable to encourage the children to generalise about sites. This is done by introducing the word 'site' and asking such questions as: 'Supposing you were choosing a site for an airstrip on our island would we consider the same things as when choosing a home?'

The kind of conclusion you hope they will reach is 'when you choose a site you have to take into consideration a number of different things — exactly what they are will depend on the kind of site it is — one of them is usually how near it is to things people need.' The teacher may well ask why children should be encouraged to form such general understandings and articulate them in conversation. First, we would say that people generalise spontaneously on the basis of their day-to-day experience. 'Dogs bite' is a useful generalisation and the child who has learned it can apply it in future in his dealings with dogs. Similarly if children form generalisations about sites (or anything else) they can transfer and apply the generalisation the next time they encounter sites — possibly in secondary school geography but also in such day-to-day tasks as choosing where to live.

Teaching the Concept of Communication

Here again the teacher needs a motivating device. He can interest the children with a brief story of how a boat is seen on the horizon and the children try to attract its attention. Possible tasks include listing various means of communication (flags, fire, morse code, flashing lights, messages in bottles). The teacher then discusses with the children how a message to be signalled will differ from a message put in a bottle for the children's parents. They may suggest that the signalled message must be brief. If it is for a visible boat then it may not need to say much about the children's whereabouts. If it is a radio message or a message for the children's parents one of the main problems will be communicating their whereabouts. How can this be done? Here the teacher may or may not find it helpful to introduce the use of a globe and show the marks of latitude and longitude. These will not be fully understood by the children but they can see how useful they would be for identifying one's position. Notions like northern and southern hemisphere may also emerge. The children can also be asked what the parents will most want to hear? Since they will want to know that the children are safe, all the names must be included. What would be wrong with a message such as: 'We are shipwrecked on a desert island'? One would hope the children would criticise this message for lack of a date, lack of indication of where the island is, and who is shipwrecked and so on. The idea of communication can be further developed by suggesting that the message in the bottle might reach people who did not know English. Can they record their story in pictures and put the pictures into a bottle?

Exercise 6

Make up some activities or tasks, on communication arising from an encounter with a native tribe. Write a little story which introduces these.

Other possibilities include: problems which arise when two groups of children are separated; what kinds of information might they need to communicate? A possible response might be good news (sighting a ship) and bad news (enemies). Another group of tasks might involve interpreting messages, e.g. a friendly tribe send a message in pictures but what exactly does it mean?

Exercise 7

Make up such a 'message' — one which would be easy to interpret, another more difficult.

Teaching Concepts and Understandings about Groups and Decision Making

While desert island lends itself to producing problems of a technological character, it is not desirable that all the children's problem-solving activities should be of that kind. Social studies are essentially concerned with developing understandings about the behaviour of human beings in groups. Children have considerable experience of being members of groups, the family, the class and the peer group. The desert island situation gives them a chance to explore the situation where there is a leaderless peer group and where this group has to remake all the major decisions about group living. To take a simple exercise: the teacher poses the question: 'Do we all live in one large house, or do we each have separate small houses, or do we live with a group of friends?' Here we can draw on children's experiences of having or not having a room of their own. They should be able to list the advantages and the draw-backs of each way of living. In the same context they can examine how they reach a conclusion on this matter. Do they all spontaneously and immediately agree on one of the three alternatives; is there a division of opinion; are there more children in favour of one alternative than another; did people change their minds in the process of discussion, being persuaded by the arguments of other members of the group? This examination of decision making may allow the teacher to introduce vocabulary such as majority, minority, vote and election.

Exercise 8

Make up some other little story which may introduce the matter of decision making and related vocabulary. Think up some questions to act as props for less able children.

When the children first made their list of what they would need to survive on the island, one of them mentioned a leader and another 'someone experienced'. Either of these suggestions or the problems arising from decision making may introduce the notion of leadership.

What are the understandings we want to develop about leadership? One is that leaders need certain qualities, another that they need the support and co-operation of those they lead, a third that leaders may abuse their authority, and so on. To consider the qualities required by a leader first. Here the teacher or the children may pose the prob-lem: 'What sort of person do we choose as leader? Do we choose the oldest, the biggest or the cleverest? Which of these words describe a good leader? — timid, brave, rude, unkind, tactful, good tempered, obedient, etc.'

Exercise 9

Make up your own list of adjectives. Then go on to write three or four sentences about three characters, Kate, Bill and Trevor. Make your character sound like real boys and girls and give one of them the qualities of a good leader. Ask the children which they think would be best as a leader. Tell them to give their reasons. For a harder exercise give each character some strengths and some weaknesses and write rather more about each. Let three of the children pretend to be the characters, each telling the others why he or she should be chosen as a leader. Try as a final task to devise some questions that get children to generalise about leadership (see page 176).

Exercise 10

Take one or more of the following understandings about leadership and devise a way of developing it:

(1) that leaders may abuse their authority.
(2) that leaders may be overthrown by force.
(3) that leaders depend on the support of the group.

A final point, it does not seem wise to ask the children to choose a leader from among themselves. Such a procedure does not permit a frank discussion of the qualities of a good leader and if the children point out each other's strengths and weaknesses of character, feelings may well be hurt. Hence our suggestion that the teacher 'distances' the situation by using imaginary characters and roleplay.

Many of the problems which arise in the desert island situation involve relationships between people. Some of these may be best developed via drama and discussion rather than by written tasks. For example quite early in the simulation the question of sex-roles may arise. One group of children decided they wished to live in two houses one for boys and one for girls 'since boys and girls preferred to be on their own'. A problem then arises about work. Do both groups expect that the girls will do the cleaning and cooking and the boys the hunting and exploring? Even if they do, it may well be useful if the teacher postulates a situation where the girls rebel against their traditional role. The teacher can make up a story to illustrate this . . . which ends 'Jane says it isn't fair that she should have to clean up after the boys, and anyway she is a much better swimmer than any of the boys, she would rather go exploring and hunting'. When the story is introduced and stopped part way through the children can be asked to set out what follows introducing appropriate dialogue.

Exercise 11

Make up a similar story which could lead into drama, e.g. one member of the group won't do his share of the work . . . the children act out the situation and attempt to solve it dramatically.

Notes on Exercises

Exercise 1

David has not produced many ideas – though five is not a bad effort. They are all 'concrete'. He has listed things to do rather than needs. The last item shows some confusion but he has used the word survivors in an appropriate place.

Helpful comments might be: 'This is an interesting list of things we could do on the island. Which of these things would help us to keep warm? You could put those two together couldn't you? What sort of food would you get by climbing trees? What else would you need to stay alive? Tell me some more about the last thing on your list.'

Exercise 2

The main characteristics of money are:
(1) portability
(2) durability
(3) not easily forged
(4) within agreed fixed value
(5) not easily available
(6) easily identifiable
(7) established by authority or agreement

Possible Questions – Look at our coins and paper money:
Why are they small?
Why do they have those particular words and pictures on them?
Are there any disadvantages in having money made of paper?
What problems would you have if you tried to make some imitation money?
Why do we have a lot of coins of different values?
What would be the disadvantages of having one value only?

Exercise 3

Possible Questions

3.1 What will be the best time to do the hard work while we are on the island?

What will be the best time during the day to have a rest?

What kind of roof shall we need on our shelter?

How can we make sure we always have enough water to drink?

When shall we go to bed (remember we have no lights).

What sort of clothes will we need?

Will we need fires?

3.2 Item of information about the arctic that might be included:

(1) the sea freezes over in the winter.

(2) there are no trees.

(3) the only animals about are seals which live under the ice.

(4) it is dark nearly all the time in winter.

Here is a picture of the Arctic. It has a very harsh climate (word previously introduced).

What shall we eat?

What can we use for clothes?

What work shall we do?

What can we make our houses of?

Will we need lights?

What can we use to keep warm?

Exercise 6

Possible tasks could include:

(1) You meet a group of natives for the first time. How do you show you are friendly? (Possible responses here would include – smiling, friendly gestures, offers of presents).

(2) The natives have some fish which you would like. How do you convey that you want it, are willing to trade and offer something?

(3) You want to find out where the natives live. How can you make them understand? When you have thought this out try it on some other children and see if they can understand you. (Possible responses will go beyond gestures to pictures in sand, etc.)

This may be elaborated with other variants, e.g.

Where did you catch the fish?

'Who' questions could be added – who is the boss around here?

The children may be led to perceive that 'why' questions are the hardest to convey by gestures or signs.

Exercise 8

Some suggestions

(1) There is only a certain amount of wood. Do the shipwrecked children try to build a boat to escape from the island or do they settle down to living on the island and use the wood to build a house?

   Here the children ought to list the arguments on both sides. It would be possible to introduce role-play here. One or two children have a card telling them to argue for leaving the island, one or two are given a card with arguments for staying . . . each side has to try to persuade the rest of the children to vote for its side.

(2) A group of three children are out hunting and exploring. A boy sprains his ankle badly. The problem confronting the group is what they are going to do. Who is going for help? Who is going to stay behind with the injured child, or are they going to leave him while they go for help?

Exercise 9

A possible illustration:

Bill is very good with his hands and can make all kinds of things but he does not enjoy playing games much. He is rather homesick and wishes very much that he was with his parents again. Sometimes the other children think he is moody.

Trevor always enjoys life. He is very good at football and makes other children laugh. He is rather lazy however and hates getting up in the morning or having to carry water.

Kate is very energetic and really gets on with anything she has to do. She is friendly with all the rest of the children and they will usually do what she suggests.

Questions to encourage generalisations about leadership:

What sort of person would make a good leader or soldier?
What sort of person would make a good football captain?
What sort of person would make a good leader on a desert island?
Do you always need the same sort of person as a leader? (Children reach the conclusion that the qualities needed in a leader will vary according to the job he has to do.)
Which of the following are needed by all leaders: courage, tact, kindness, good temper, the ability to remain calm in difficult moments, skill in playing games, physical strength, good eyesight,

a sense of humour, the ability to do sums.
What qualities (explain word) are needed by all leaders?

(1) John was made leader and had to share out the food. He kept the biggest pineapple for himself and gave the next biggest to his friend.
   What would the other children feel?
   What could they do? (complain, turn him out).
   What makes him a bad leader?
   What makes a bad leader in the following instances – distributing food, distributing duties, distributing chores?

(2) John is the leader and he has the three biggest boys on his side. They are lazy and won't work and if the other children complain they thump them. What can the other children do about this? (possible responses include: they can gang up against the four or persuade them to behave differently or go away and live somewhere else without them).

Exercise 11

Possibilities

   (1) Trevor, who is the elected leader, begins to get very bossy. He orders people about and becomes a bit of a bully . . .
   (2) The children find a footprint in the sand on a remote beach . . .
   (3) The children, lost and hungry, encounter a group of natives who are frightened of them and run away. How can they make it plain that they don't mean any harm and want some help?

Modern children do not have many opportunities to watch people
doing productive work. If children of five and six are asked to draw
pictures of people working they show the jobs they have had a chance
to observe like the work of the milkmen, the dustman, the bus conductor, the nurse or the doctor. Even when they know what work
their fathers do they are often very uncertain about what is involved.
The children of affluent middle-class suburbs whose fathers work in
managerial and administrative positions may have less understanding
of what their fathers' work involves than children whose parents are
lorry drivers or shop assistants. Different communities, too, provide
different opportunities to learn about people's work. In a mining
village nearly every child in the class had a father who was a miner
and some of them had little understanding of what he did; in a com-
muter village hardly any one at all works in the community itself and
children may be similarly ignorant. A good first move for a teacher
therefore is to consider what informal education the children in his
class have already had and in what kind of community they are living.
A second step may be to plan a visit or series of visits to help to fill the
gaps in children's experience, e.g. children familiar only with service
occupations, often covered by topics in infant schools on 'people who
help us', ought perhaps to have a visit to some workplace where food
or goods are produced – to a farm, a bakery, a building site, a factory.
A visit of this kind is likely to be attractive to children, who spontaneously spend a lot of time watching parents working or watching
men making holes in the road and can become a nuisance to builders
on a building site.

Before organising such a visit, it may be worth considering exactly
what understandings about people and work it may be intended to
cultivate. In doing so, we are seeking to identify the attributes of the
concept of work. Most seven-year-olds are quite familiar with the word
'work' and can use it accurately in an appropriate context. As we have
said, many five-year-olds can draw a picture of someone working if
asked to do so: they can give an example of the concept, a major test
of understanding. With 'work' therefore we have to go further and ask
such questions as 'What is it for?' The answer to this is two-pronged:
one prong to lead to the function of work in the family economy and

in the life of the individual, the other to its place in the economy, in the production of goods and services. If we start to list the understandings the children are going to learn we may start as follows:

people work to make money for themselves and their families
people work for other reasons too e.g.
interest, company, status

and add:

many different workers help to produce
any type of goods etc.

Exercise

Can you think of any other understandings about work which we may need to cultivate in children?

Answer: workers are usually specialists because that is most efficient
(specialisation of labour),
machinery can reduce the amount of work to be done,
some jobs take a long time to learn and are highly skilled:
others are learned quickly and are less skilled.
Whether an activity is work or play may depend on how you
feel about it or whether it is paid.

In planning the visit, we need to focus attention on the people who work at the workplace, the different jobs they do, their role in producing the food or goods, the machines they use and the measures taken to ensure their safety since all workplaces, including kitchens at home, can be dangerous places. On the return to the classroom the teacher may ask the children to list the jobs observed. Different children may be asked to illustrate by drawings each of the most important jobs together with the equipment used and these can be arranged in the order of their contribution to the end product; the pictures might show the driver of the bulldozer clearing the ground, the bricklayer putting in foundations, the cement mixer and its operation, producing cement for the floors, the lorry driver bringing the bricks, the crane driver lifting the scaffolding, etc. If the children have made relevant visits in connection with other topics, they may be asked to make a similar sequence of pictures for, say, the farm, the post office or the bakery. Alternatively the school itself may provide a contrasting example. What different jobs are done by people at school. Why do they each take one particular job? Why doesn't the teacher break off to answer the phone or cook the dinner or stoke the boiler? We hope that ideas like efficiency and skill would emerge. Eventually the understandings which the children reach may be summarised, e.g. 'Each person does one job so that he can do it really well' or 'Every different kind of worker helps to build the block of offices' (or bake the bread or grow the food). The children then write this as a caption to go with the pictures. It could be expressed in the words agreed jointly by the children and the teacher.

If the teacher wishes to reinforce the notion of specialisation of labour there is a short American film produced for six/seven-year-olds which uses a story about prehistoric men to teach this concept,[1] or the teacher could introduce a story about 'Long, long ago when the hunter had to make all his weapons, hunt the animal, haul it back, skin it, make its skin into clothes, build his shelter, etc.', and how helpful he found it when, he, who was a very good hunter indeed but not very good at making weapons, found a friend who was very skilful at making knives but hated hunting in the cold and the wet.

A further development from the visit may involve a consideration of the function of tools, machinery and power in relation to work. If this needs justification in terms of children's interests we have only to look at the wide range of children's toys which involve miniatures of adult working equipment; tip-up lorries, toy telephones and typewriters, space suits, nurses' uniforms, model farms, etc. The children are invited to list the equipment they observed on the visit, in small groups of 6-8 children, and then to discuss how each item helps the workers. It will emerge that there is a distinction between tools and powered machinery. The children if questioned should be able to distinguish between these: the hand tools which may be more efficient than the worker's hands, and the powered equipment which may replace the labour of many men for many days. The groups of children may then be asked to list the equipment used in other places they have observed — or if necessary be set to find out from books. Each child can be asked to find out what machines they have at home which help their mothers with the work and what other machines real or imagined she would like to have to help her. We should soon have listed on the blackboard or on large sheets of paper machinery and equipment used in the home, the school, the farm, the bakery, the building site, etc. The same lists may be regrouped according to the type of power used: petrol, electricity. The notion of what is economically justified may emerge: why is a duplicator necessary in school but not at home, why does the school have a floor-polisher

but hardly any homes do? Why do some people use the laundrette
rather than have a washing machine?

Older children can be asked in groups to discuss a list of what makes
machines useful, e.g. they work faster, they do not get tired, they
sometimes do a job better (e.g. sewing machines make neater stitches),
they save time and journeys (telephones) etc. The children can then be
asked if there are any drawbacks, e.g. they cost a lot to buy, they use
power, they break down, they can be dangerous, they wear out.

Understandings about the functions of machinery may be further
reinforced by focusing attention on the past. The children can be asked
to question their grandmothers about how the work of the home was
done in her childhood. Or they may interview someone of the appropriate age-group in school. How was the washing done? How was the
house lit and warmed? How much work was involved? Who did it?

If we turn our attention to peoples' experience of work a simple
first step is to ask the children to list, in groups, all the jobs they know
and then for the teacher to make a comprehensive list on the board. He
or she then asks them to group the jobs that 'go together'. The children
may start by grouping jobs according to function 'nurses or doctors'
working in hospitals, 'farmers or bakers' producing food, etc. The
teacher then might suggest they look at other possible groupings by
asking, 'Which jobs are dangerous?' 'Which mean working at night?'
'Which take a very long time to learn?' 'Which mean telling other people
what to do?' 'Which mean getting dirty?' 'Which mean you have got to
wear special clothes?' 'Which people make things?' 'Which people do
not make things but provide a service to other people as bus drivers do?'
It may be useful with abler or older children to introduce words like
'authority', 'responsibility', 'goods' and 'services' and encourage them
to use these words in speech and in writing in the context of this
exercise.

The next step is to encourage the children to find out more about
specific jobs either from books, using the techniques already recommended in Chapter 5, or by interviewing people — or indeed by a combina-
tion of both methods. If the children are to conduct interviews, they
need to practise — perhaps upon some member of staff or a parent —
before they go on to question some invited member of the public such
as a visiting policeman. (It is as well to tell them that people don't like
to be asked how much they earn!) They should have had enough prep-
aration by this stage to have a rough idea of what questions to ask and
should compose, with help, their own class questionnaire. It is wise to
limit the number of questions and, if it is proposed to quantify the

responses, possibly to record them on a block graph, a considerable number of the questions should require yes/no answers. To help the children frame the questions the teacher can provide an example of both a 'closed' and an open question on work: 'Is your work interesting?' and 'Would you like to change your work?' Each child can be asked to compose at least one question and then the best ten or twelve can be selected. If a question is badly framed, ask the child to say what kind of answer they expect to get. In addition the questions can be used experimentally on one of your colleagues or a co-opera-tive parent, and if the children find any question is not understood they can be encouraged to change it. Also to be considered is the task of recording the answers. Yes/no answers do not present any great difficulty but open-ended questions are more problematic. It does not matter if the children find it difficult to make a note of the answer to the open-ended questions. As long as there are only one or two of these they are likely to remember what they are told, especially if a group of children are present at each interview. Even if the children do not go outside the group represented by their own parents and the people who work in the school, they should increase their under-standing of what people feel about work.

One value of having a number of children use the same set of ques-tions, but interviewing different people or using different books on different occupations, is that when they have collected the information, it can be discussed and likenesses and contrasts identified. It may emerge that while some jobs can be learned very quickly others take years of apprenticeship or as a student. In the process of making comparisons the children will be learning to make generalisations e.g. 'People work to make money which they need to buy things with' but they should also learn to modify the generalisations by saying 'most people . . .' or 'some people' or 'nearly every one'. If 'generalising' sounds rather hard for primary children, remember we do it in quite simple statements e.g. 'Dogs bark'. The important thing about these generalisations is that the children are making them about the behaviour of groups of people after making a serious investigation. Alternatively, after the investigation, the teacher can provide a series of statements about work and say 'Are these true?' 'What makes you think they are true?'

Not all children entering primary school understand why people work. They usually know they work for money and that their fathers give them pocket money from the money earned. Quite often however they do not understand how the family economy works. Their lack of

understanding and the belief that their parents' resources are infinite
creates friction when mothers impatiently tell them that she cannot
buy toys or icecream every time she goes to the shops. It may be helpful to make up a short story round this situation and leading to the
making of a list of all the things the family spends money on. If this is
done we should not assume that the family is of the kind usually considered to be dominant, with father providing mother with house-
keeping money. Different groups have different practices: in some
northern households, the women traditionally handle all the money.
And in many households today there are two incomes since many
married women work while in a substantial minority the chief wage
earner is a woman. There is a danger in topics of this kind of reinforcing
stereotypes or reflecting a social situation already dated. Investigating
the books available for children to use on the subject of 'work', we find
there are few enough descriptions of women's work and where they
exist they reflect women in jobs traditionally female, e.g. 'Mother is a
social worker'. In inviting people into school to talk about their jobs
try to include either a woman in a responsible post or from an occupation traditionally male, say a bus driver.

A further exercise of value is for the children to try to decide for
themselves how important specific jobs are and why. This can be linked
to the question of wages: who should be paid most and why? We can
give either individually or collectively the following list — or any other
variant on it.

Dustman
Pop star
Policeman
Train driver
Doctor
Miner
Bus driver

We know that average seven-year-olds from schools on an urban
working-class estate can apply the concept of importance in a context
similar to this. One could for example say that the doctor was important because 'he knows best', a reference to his specialised knowledge.
We can ask children rather older to weigh the claims of dangerous as
opposed to dirty jobs, jobs which attract popular acclaim to jobs which
carry responsibility for life and death. The children can be asked to discuss this in small groups and repeat their agreed list in order of

importance to the other children who can question them about their decisions. It is not a good idea however to push children either in a group or a class to reach a consensus. One of the things to be learned here is that people do not necessarily agree about this.

This does not of course exhaust the possibilities of the topic. Other children (9-11) might be asked to look at the jobs advertised in the local paper and list the work available in the locality. In Nottingham they would come up with jobs in hosiery, lace, tailoring, mining, chemicals and engineering apart from those common to most districts. They could go on to consider what a job advertisement should tell you and possibly to decide what might constitute a 'good' job. They could look at a map of their own locality and label the sites of the major factories and what people did in them. Perhaps you yourself can suggest other possibilities?

Notes

1. 'Why People Have Special Jobs: The Man Who Made Spinning Tops.' This film is part of the series *Basic Concepts in Social Studies*, made by the Learning Corporation of America and distributed by Rank, 1970. It can be obtained from the National Audio Visual Aids Film Library, code no. 21.9031.

The Teacher's Own Knowledge

For the purpose of discussing this topic, we will assume that the reader knows the following pieces of information about North America and about North American Indians:

(1)   that North America can be divided very roughly into three clima-tic/vegetation/cultural zones: 'woodland' in the east and on the Pacific coast, grassland or 'great plains' in the centre of the continent and 'desert' in the south-west.

(2)   that each of these zones supported distinctive pre-European Indian cultures.

(3)   that at the time of the early European incursions into North America, the eastern woodland zone was the scene of fierce and largely successful wars of conquest waged by a group of Indian tribes called the Iroquois.

(4)   that in the thirteenth century flourishing farming cultures in the south-west were struck by dramatic climate changes which turned the area from fertile grassland into its present condition of desert.

(5)   that during the late seventeenth and early eighteenth centuries the tribes of the Great Plains tamed horses, which had strayed up from Mexico, having been introduced into North America by the Spaniards in the sixteenth century.

(6)   that all the Indian cultures of North America were destroyed, or reduced to vestiges of their former selves by the coming of Europeans.

All this information is easily accessible, and must be possessed by the teacher if 'Red Indians' is to be approached, planned and presented as a topic at a worthwhile level, for children of junior age.

Obviously, it would be fruitless to approach this topic equipped only with un-organised cultural baggage, as it were, even though in this particular case our cultural baggage is very extensive, because of films and television -- wigwam, pipe of peace, mustang, scalping, Apache, and dozens of other words and ideas have some sort of meaning for us, or are at least vaguely familiar to just about everybody, because of films, but we would rightly feel insecure about embarking on this topic equipped only with 'what everybody knows' by way of knowledge about Indians. But how much must we know? To demand that we know when the Minnesota Sioux moved onto the Great Plains, or the dates of the Seminole Wars would take us into realms of specialised knowledge, when one of our main arguments is that specialised knowledge, although very helpful, is not essential to intelligent treatment of social studies topics.

The best rule is probably this: that we need to know enough about a topic to decide which important, transferable concepts that topic might be used to foster, and also enough to make a provisional judgement about which parts of the topic to emphasise in order to develop the concepts most effectively. Beyond that essential minimum we can acquire all the information we like (and if we expect our class to be moved to find out a lot of information, we might reasonably expect that we ourselves might be similarly moved), while retaining an alertness about our areas of ignorance. This 'alertness' must show itself in discrimination about what to do when our ignorance is revealed. Suppose Jean asks 'Where did the Arapahoe live?' and Terry asks 'It says here that the Sioux didn't always try to kill people in battles they just tried to touch them – they called it "counting coup" – why did they do that?' In both cases the answer might be 'I don't know' but the response to Jean will be 'Look it up' or 'Let's look it up', while to Terry we should obviously be saying 'Let's have a think about this', because he has come up with something that might have a bearing on central concepts such as 'way of life', 'environment affects people's ways of life and ideas', which are the concepts that we have very probably set up as goals for our study of 'Red Indians' anyway.

Teaching the Topic on 'Red Indians'

The topic will be presented in a relatively detailed way, in order to illustrate further how the ideas of planning through objectives, and in particular, of using concepts as a planning framework (ideas presented in outline on pp. 158-61), might be used in practice. The apparent precision of the planning will unavoidably be artificial to a certain extent: we will have to assume that each session goes approximately as planned – a very large assumption! The alternative, however, would have been to present a very complicated and long account of the progress of a large number of individual children through this topic, with all their partial failures, qualified successes, blind alleys, improvisions, etc.

'Red Indians' can be looked at in several different, equally legitimate and interesting ways. They can be seen as classic cases of losers in a conflict; of victims of oppression; as excellent instances of a people whose history has been presented largely by their enemies, with consequent distortions; and so on. This particular set of plans springs however from an interest by the teacher in North American Indians as vivid exemplars of human adaptation to a great range of different physical environments within one continent. The imagination is particularly struck by two dramatic events, the great drought of *circa* 1280, which wrecked the agriculture-based culture of the Indians of the south-west, and the transformation of the life of the Plains Indians in the seventeenth/eighteenth centuries by their 'discovery' of the horse. The white man, as such, only hovers on the fringes of this conceptual picture. This basic decision about the emphasis of the topic must be taken before we can write our 'paragraph at adult level' (see page 161) which will produce our list of concept-objectives. The paragraph itself might look like this:

> The Indians lived in a lot of different <u>environments</u>. This <u>led</u> to them having different <u>ways of life,</u> particularly it determined whether they were <u>nomadic</u> or <u>settled agricultural</u> people (though they all lived in <u>tribal</u> forms of organisation). There are some dramatic instances of the <u>impact of change</u> in their environment on their ways of life, e.g. change in <u>climate.</u>

This gives a list of eight concept-objectives, the only one of which in need of comment is '<u>led</u>' an innocuous word which obviously conceals the important concept of causation. We might in fact say that a 'key' question to ask in a study of any human group and its relationship to its environment is: 'Were, or are, these people able to modify their environment, and thereby their culture, or were they able only to respond to their environment?' In this particular case, the environment firmly moulded the ways of life, and so the mechanism of this 'moulding', 'causing' or 'leading to' is a thing which it is vital for the children to understand.

We still have some important planning decisions to take. First, given a realistic time span of five or six weeks for this topic, which Indians are we going to learn about? Obviously the destructive drought of the thirteenth century and its effect in the south-west will figure, and the Plains Indians will be prominent because of the dramatic impact of the horse. They will also be prominent for another, operational reason, in that they are the Indians that already interest most children, and most writers of books for children. When it comes to woodland Indians, though, there are several different groups, all interesting in different ways. Perhaps the best way would be to use the diversity of woodland Indians to allow children to do individual research on particular groups?

We now have the embryo of a plan:

(i) South-western Indians. (1 week)
(ii) Woodland Indians (children to work on *either* Pacific Coast Indians *or* Eastern Woodland Indians, in groups?). (2 weeks)
(iii) Plains Indians. (2 weeks)

A preliminary run-through a plan for a first session on the ancient South-western Indians being dispersed by a great drought, throws up some difficulties. To understand the story, the children would have to understand at least the following things – that climate can change, that plants won't grow without water, that in a drought, game animals move away as the grass withers and, the most important idea of all, that if a community switches from agriculture to hunting and gathering as a means of gaining food, it must disperse, it cannot live in large settlements like the great south-western cliff-dwellings. In other words, if we use concept-objectives as a planning guide, one of the questions we must ask is how many concepts which may be a source of difficulty are involved in any one learning-session, especially in the first learning experiences of a new topic, where the tone is set and the confidence of both teacher and children either established or undermined.

In this particular case, we have displaced the South-western Indians from the start of the topic (although they would have made a dramatic and interesting opening), simply by reason of the number and difficulty of the learning objectives involved in their study. The wisest course might now be to put the Woodland Indians at the beginning, to establish the relatively simple relationship between environment and life-style, before we go into the problems caused by environmental change.

The first phase of work on Woodland Indians could hinge on questions related to picture I. Broad general questions such as 'How are these Indians different to the ones you see on TV' will serve as a rough 'pre-test' on the question of children's pre-existing perceptions of Indians, which may range from total identification of 'Indian' with 'Plains Indians' to a fair knowledge of Woodland Indians arising from the fact that TV happens to be doing 'The Last of the Mohicans', to a total confusion as revealed by this little piece on Indians (spelling corrected) 'They used to hunt buffalo and they would go in the woods and ambush the redcoats and the other Indians the Apaches was the worst'.

Picture I

The central ideas of the environment, lifestyle, agriculture and climate can be addressed by questions like:

'Think how many things they could use wood for?'

'What tools would they need to live in the forest?'

'What tools would they need if they were going to plant things and grow them?'

'What is it called when people grow crops to eat?'

'Why do you think they grow things — Why not just hunt animals?'

'Look at their clothes and houses — what do you think the climate was like there?'

Our rough impression of pupils' understanding of some of the topics main concepts can be confirmed by questions on books, such as the following, *Red Indians* (J.C. Gagg, Blackwells 'Little Learning Library, 1974, pp. 8-9).

All Indians had to find food. Most of them hunted animals.

They used bows and arrows, knives, clubs, traps, axes and blowguns.

They caught deer, bears, rabbits and other small animals.

Many Indians caught fish in rivers.

Some caught them with their hands, while others used pointed spears.

Some fished with hooks made of bone.

Many tribes of Indians, of course, also grew some of their food.

Questions

(1) What other animals might they catch to eat?

(2) What other things besides food might they hunt animals for?

(3) Which do you think was the best way to catch fish, hands, spears or hooks?

(4) Would it be better to grow food as well as hunt, or just hunt?

For abler readers, a 'scanning' exercise is possible based on *Red Indians* (T.A. Thompson, 'Blackwells' Learning Library' No. 27, 1965), which has references to Woodland Indians under 'horses', 'animals', 'hunting' and 'food'.

There are a number of more detailed aspects of the Woodland Indians' adaptation to their environment which can be profitably explored, for instance quite precise problems such as why they made canoes from birch-bark instead of hollowing out tree-trunks, what crops they grew which have since been introduced to Europe, their experiments with irrigation, their forms of money and what they needed them for. Research exercises on say the Florida and Pacific Coast Indians, (both fairly well documented in standard junior level treatments of

Indians) can reinforce the environment-lifestyle link. The whole study of the Woodland Indians would lend itself well to summary in various forms, e.g. a frieze or a descriptive 'letter' from an explorer or, for less able writers, a list of features of life common to, say, East Coast and Pacific Coast Woodland dwellers.

Ideas not yet tackled are *nomadic* and 'impact of change' and *tribal*, which could reasonably be left over to the 'Plains Indians' phase. However, an aspect of Woodland Indian life which has not been touched on is warfare, and especially the conquests of the Iroquois confederation.

The pertinent question to ask here is, could learning about these things help to illuminate some or all of our target concepts? In this case, the answer is 'yes', up to a point. The particular skills of woodland warfare, e.g. ambushes and the construction of stockades will make an interesting subject in themselves, and also will illustrate the central idea of adaptation of way of life to environment and make a good contrast with the very different light-cavalry skills of the Plains Indians. As to the particular matter of the Iroquois, that could be used to illuminate the concept of 'tribe', but it would be a left-handed example, in that the Iroquois confederation was in fact an attempt to transcend the tribal structure of society, so the characteristics of a 'tribe' might be much more handily dealt with through some Plains example than through the Iroquois. The final judgement therefore, is that work on warfare is included, but no particular attempt will be made to teach about the Iroquois, dominant as they were, historically, in the story of the eastern Woodland tribes.

This is not, of course, the only possible decision about warfare in general and the Iroquois in particular, but it illustrates two important things about planning through concept objectives. First, it is wise to pause now and then to check whether our objectives are being covered, and if they are not, to check that our plans for the later parts of the topic will leave room for them. Secondly, we must note that we cannot plan by a short list of concept objectives alone. Warfare, and Iroquois warfare, were very prominent features of Woodland life, and we would do violence to the truth if we left children with the impression that Woodlands Indians sat about all day peacefully adjusting to their environment. What we have to do is neither add bits in to the topic, because, like Everest, 'they are there', regardless of how they contribute to our learning goals, nor leave out important matters because they do not fit our master-plan. We have to compromise, and this particular decision on warfare and the Iroquois, is offered as an example of a reasonable compromise on this kind of question.

Plains Indians

We can adopt a problem-solving approach to the 'pre-horse' Plains
Indians which will link with and reinforce the learning achieved in the
Woodland Indians phase of the topic. We can ask the children to work
out a way of life for the Indians, taking into account the virtual absence
of trees, the difficulty of growing crops and the positive factor of the
presence of big, but wandering, herds of buffalo. Through stories, and
pictures like J, we can get children to write and draw about the central
problem of hunting large, strong animals on foot. This will set us up for
dealing with one of the most romantic and interesting episodes in the
history of mankind in North America – the 'discovery' of the horse by
the Plains Indians and the consequent transformation of their way of
life.

Picture J

As well as making the obvious points about how the horse would
enable the Indians both to follow and to hunt the buffalo herds more
efficiently, we should try to explore important sub-areas of the general

idea 'change in way of life' such as education, wealth, warfare, social
status and the tribe as a social unit and communications. The following
sets of tasks show how we might get into these areas and avoid the
temptation to work at a descriptive and relatively trivial level, temptation which is very strong just as this point precisely because the details
of Plains Indian life are so instrinsically interesting.

Set Task A (more able children)
  (1) What kind of things would a Plains Indian boy have to learn?
       Who do you think would teach him? Read *A Closer Look at
       Plains Indians* by A. Davis, Hamilton, 1977, from page 18 and
       check your answers.
  (2) If someone said a Plains Indian was 'rich', what do you think
       that would mean?
  (3) Do you think there would be more fighting, or less, between the
       Indians, after they got the horses? What do you think the
       Indians might fight about?
  (4) An Indian called Blue Feather wanted to be an important man in
       his tribe. Make up a story about how he might have tried to do
       it.
  (5) Draw the story of a raid on an enemy tribe the way the Indians
       used to draw it. (Look at page 9 *A Closer Look at Plains Indians*
       for ideas.) Why do you think the Indians drew stories like that?

Set Task B (less able children)
  (1) Read page 12 of *Red Indians* (Blackwells Little Learning Library)
       and see what Indian boys had to learn. What other things do you
       think they had to learn?
  (2) Which of these things would an Indian most like to have:
       (i) a lot of tepees,
       (ii) a lot of horses,
       (iii) a lot of beads.
  (3) What do you think the Indians might have fought each other
       about?
  (4) What things would an Indian do to make people think he was
       brave? Draw a picture-story of an Indian doing a brave thing.
  (5) Look at the picture of Indians sending smoke signals. What might
       the signals be about?

The role of women among the Plains Indians ought to be investigated as
well, and contrasts drawn by the children with their role in the agricultural

Woodland system, and a very interesting psychological study can be based round this question: 'Why would an Indian risk getting killed in a battle just to touch an enemy with a stick' ('counting coup'). Whatever aspects of Plains Indian life are investigated, though, the final piece of work, whether it be a drama, frieze or some piece of written work would concentrate on the great changes in their way of life caused by the discovery of horses. This will pave the way for the final phase, the story of the ancient Indians of the South West.

The South-western Indians

After learning something of the connection between climate, crops and lifestyle in the previous two phases, and after a long exploration of the idea of radical change of way of life in the case of Plains Indians we can now tackle the question of the great south-western drought with more confidence, and in fact use it as a sort of 'post-test' of some of the growth in understanding we have been seeking.

Stage A

The children are told that long ago some Indians lived lives very like those of the Woodland Indians except that they built 'cliff dwellings' not wooden structures. They are then told that they had a good *climate* for *agriculture* so were *settled* not *nomads*, and lived in *tribes*, and are asked to explain the italicised terms.

Then through a story, the children are told how the rain stopped for over twenty years, and asked 'What would happen?' If the cardinal points of crop-destruction and dispersal of game are not made, then the teacher must explain them. If the concrete effects of drought are understood, then discussion-drama is a very good medium for exploring the social effects: the children, in the role of the Indians, deciding what to do — migrate, stay put and hope for the best, change their way of life in some way, stick together or disperse. Some real-life answers to these problems have shown a great range of level of understanding:

Child A 'We can't live here anymore, its a desert soon. If only we had somethings like horses we could go up to the plains and hunt buffalo. We would take a long time to learn it but we would be happy there and no different ways of life. But if we just walk it will be no good and most of us will die.'

Apart from attributing extraordinary historical prescience to an Indian of 1275 this response is very apt indeed.

Child B represents the other extreme: 'Save up some corn and keep it in the ground seven years and plant it in the sand'. This response represents perhaps a muddled recollection of the story of Joseph in Egypt, but does not face the problem of the environment-lifestyle relationship at all. Most responses to the problem go for an abandonment of settled life, and the adoption of some sort of nomadic life of hunting and gathering, showing a grasp of the main idea and sometimes some very imaginative perceptions of the fear and reluctance with which such a change would be undertaken.

The most difficult idea, in practice, which children seem to encounter with this particular problem is the need for dispersal, the idea that groups of six or seven hundred people cannot wander round a desert living on roots and lizards. It would be an interesting exercise to try with your own children: in this Indian context, or some other setting, how can you promote the idea that hunting and gathering cultures necessarily involve a very low population density? It is an intriguing problem, especially where children read that 'thousands' of Indians gathered at the Battle of Little Bighorn, which brings home in dramatic fashion that we have to separate the ideas of 'population' and 'population density'.

To return to general themes, though, the response to the problem of the south-western drought of the thirteenth century will show up fairly well whether the topic has been successfully addressing its concept-objectives, or not. It is also an interesting and worthwhile problem in itself and so enables us to end the topic quite elegantly, as it were, with a 'test' that does not look like a test. Also, if interest is still high, and we feel justified in so doing, the topic can now go quite naturally beyond its intended span and set of objectives, and consider the impact of Europeans on Indian cultures.

One of the problems which plagues junior teachers is lack of suitable reading material for children. Some areas are well provided for, 'Red Indians' being a case in point, but in other areas, the provision is much thinner. One answer is to make your own. The following story (pp. 200-4) about a football team was one which we have ourselves made up. As you will see, it is not very long, and required no great literary talent to write – any teacher could do the same. The great positive merit of 'home-made' reading materials is that they can be written in such a way as to form a good basis for whatever skills and concepts the teacher wants to develop. If you turn to page 205 and look at 'Tasks – A' you will see that tasks 3, 5, 6, 25, 26, 28 and 29 are about mini-politics as it were, about decision making and related questions. Tasks 4, 9, 10, 11, 12 are about economics, and 13, 15, 16, 19, 21, 22, 27, 30, 32, 33, 34, 35 are about aspects of psychology, such as learning and expectation. All this is in a topic 'football', where the drive to triviality is particularly strong.

The material could be managed in various ways. The teacher could read out short passages of the story as a lead-in for work with the whole class, or get the story typed out and bound, and let a single child use it as a basis for an individual topic. (The tasks would obviously not be hurled at the child all at once, but fed out in groups of six to ten or so.) One thing the story lacks, which a commercially produced book has got in abundance is pictures. This lack is easily remedied, by getting the children themselves to make pictures, which in their turn can be used as a basis for tasks by other children. One example would be the challenge of depicting the two goals scored against South Street – one 'good' the other 'flukey'. Showing the two goals, and showing clearly which is good and which is flukey is a challenging task, and for a child, perhaps a child of a later year-group, to say which is which by a process of interpretation would be an equally interesting task.

GREENWOOD PARK RANGERS
Tony and his friends were playing football one Sunday morning in Greenwood Park. After the game, Tony had an idea.

'We could have a proper team. There are twelve of us. We could have proper shirts and everything and go in the Junior League. The kids

down South Street have a team, they play in blue and white.' Tony's
best friend Alan said 'Great! We could call the team Tigers and play
in yellow and black!' Then everybody started to talk at once – one
boy said 'No, we should play in red and white like United' another
said 'How do you join the League? We would need a teacher or somebody's dad in charge.' 'No we don't' said Alan. 'I have no football
boots' said Ginger.

So they went on saying different things, until Alan said 'Shut up!
We will have a proper meeting after dinner and decide things. It was
Tony's idea so he can be leader. He can write down all the things we
have to think about.'

So after dinner they had a meeting by the bandstand. They did not
all come, but nine did, Alan and Tony and seven others. Tony had
written the things down on paper that they had to decide about:

1. Name of team
2. What colours?
3. How to join league
4. Boots

Ginger said 'The leader should decide about team names and colours',
but Tony said 'We could all write down the name and colours we want
on a bit of paper and I will choose one of the bits with my eyes shut.'

So they did and this is what it said on the bit of paper Tony picked
up:

GREENWOOD PARK RANGERS.
ALL RED STRIP LIKE LIVERPOOL.

So that was the team name and colours now.

'How do we join the League?' asked Ginger. Alan said 'I know a boy
who plays for South Street, I will ask him how to do it.' Tony said
'Right, we put Alan in charge of finding out about joining the League.'
Ginger said 'All the proper teams have a teacher or somebody to tell
them what to do, and we should have one.'
There was a long argument about that but in the end they decided they
would try to have their team on their own, with no teachers. They
decided they would play home games in the park. Tony said he would
find out how to book a pitch.

Somebody said 'What about money for boots and things?' Alan said
'We will all buy our own' but someone else objected: 'What about balls

and things and people who can't afford boots?'

They made a list of things they might have to pay for, like this:

1. Footballs
2. Boots and Kit
3. Paying for pitch to play on
4. Paying to be in League

Then they went home to think of ways of getting money for the team. At home, Tony's dad said 'You should do it properly, put any money you get in the bank or the post-office until you need to spend it.' Tony's mother said 'You could have a supporters' club, they could run raffles and things to raise money.'

Tony's big brother Jack said 'You could all do jobs for people. You can have ten pence for a start if you will clean my bike and mend the puncture!'

So Tony cleaned the bike and did the puncture and earned the first 10p for Greenwood Park Rangers.

Tony met Alan at school on Monday, and Alan told him: 'South Street have challenged us to play them in the park on Sunday! It will have to be a friendly, of course, because we are not in the League. We can't refuse!'

So Alan and Tony got the Rangers together at dinner time and told them about the South Street challenge. 'As many as can will try to get boots, and a red shirt or anything red to wear by Sunday.' A boy called Peter said 'Who will pick the team and positions — there are fourteen of us interested now and we only want eleven.' Tony said 'I will.' But some boys said 'That's not fair, you will just pick your friends!' Then there was a big argument. Ginger had an idea 'Tony and Peter can do it together, they are in different classes so it will be fair.'

So Tony went to Peter's house that day after tea, and they picked the team, though it took a long time. Then they put a notice up at school with the team on.

Sunday came. Rangers kicked off and got a corner straight away but could not score from it.

South Street were good. There always somehow seemed to be two or three blue shirts to every red. Peter did score a good goal though, and Tony bounced a flukey goal in off his knee from a centre by Alan.

Ginger was in goal for Rangers and made some good saves. But South Street still hit six past him, so Rangers lost 6-2.

After the game Ginger looked nearly as if he might cry. Alan said 'It

wasn't Ginger's fault — our defence was terrible.' Peter said 'Yes. We
must tighten up at the back', and Tony said 'We have to get better
organised up front as well.'

One boy said 'South Street had that Mr Morris from Ashburn
School telling them what to do. We should have a teacher or somebody
to tell us.' Tony said 'No, we will coach ourselves. We will practise,
and you can get books about playing football.' 'You can't learn football
in books' said Peter, 'books are for learning facts, not how to do
things.'

'You could learn where to stand for corners and things and we could
practise taking corners and free-kicks and things like this' and Tony
started to draw a diagram in the dust.

'I think we should just play matches, that's the only way to learn'
said Peter. Everybody talked at once, then, and after a bit, they drifted
off home.

Tony talked to his brother Jack about the team's problems. 'Nobody
will agree what to do. We argue all the time. What do proper teams do?'
'They have a manager' said Jack 'He picks the team and makes the
plans.' 'What if he is no good and the team still don't win?' 'They sack
him! But he doesn't do all the jobs. They have a special man called a
"treasurer", and there is a team-captain who can shout orders in the
game itself, on the pitch.'

At the park next day, the Rangers had a vote. Tony was chosen
manager, and Peter was elected captain. But both of them only had the
jobs for the next six matches. They could be sacked if Rangers were not
winning by then. Ginger was chosen to look after the money because
he was the best at sums.

Alan found out that it was too late to join the League that season,
but they could play friendlies against teams who were in the League.
Jack told Tony how to book a pitch in the Park for them to play home
matches on.

Tony wanted Rangers to practice every day at dinner-time or after
school. Sometimes only four or five could come, so Tony made up
training things for them to do in small groups, and even things that
one boy could practice on his own.

They soon found they needed a lot more than just one football,
for all this training. Ginger told them 'We must have a bob-a-job week,
like the Scouts. Everybody must get thirty pence towards footballs
by Friday.' Peter said 'Ginger is getting too bossy.' Tony said 'People
have to be bossed about or nothing gets done.'

'You boss us around when we are training, Tony, but that is all right.

You can't let boys argue about getting into position for free-kicks and things. But Ginger should ask us to do things at home to get money, not tell us.'

'Well, he has good ideas for getting money, anyway.'

The time came for Rangers' next game, against a team called Swallows. Rangers lost 2-1, but Tony and the others were fairly happy, because the result was close. This is how Rangers got their goal. Tony had read in a football book about a way to score goals from corners. He made Rangers practice doing corners that way, and in the match they did it and it worked. Alan scored the goal. Tony was nearly as glad about that goal as if Rangers had won the game.

The next game was an away match, against a team called Riverbank. 'Away matches are harder' Tony told the Rangers 'so we want extra effort. And I want Alan to play back in the middle of the defence.' 'I like to play in mid-field and attack!'

'Well, you are our tallest player and I want you to cut out their high crosses. Swallows got both their goals from high crosses by their outside-left.'

Alan did not want to play in defence, but he said he would try, for just this one game. 'But come up in attack for corners' Tony told him. 'And we still have to keep on getting some more money!' said Ginger.

The Riverbank ground was very muddy. It was a hard game. Riverbank were fast and skilful, and the Rangers players found it hard to remember to do the things they had learned in practices. Peter shouted orders more and more, but Rangers seemed to take less and less notice. Alan kept wandering off from his place in defence.

Then Tony got the ball in the Riverbank penalty area and shot as hard as he could. The ball went in! It was the first time in their three games Rangers had ever been in the lead. Everything seemed to get easier for Rangers after that. It was the Riverside captain now who was shouting a lot. Rangers found they could remember to do their planned moves better. Alan found he quite liked playing in defence, after all. There were no more goals, but the Riverside goalkeeper had to make six good saves. Rangers walked off winners.

On the way home they passed the big ground where their local first-division team played.

'Maybe we'll have a ground like that one day and play in Division One and win the European Cup' said Ginger. Everybody laughed.

'All we did was beat Riverside 1-0!' said Peter.

'Everybody has to start somewhere!' said Ginger.

Tasks — A

1. Is it better to have a proper team or just have kick-abouts?
2. Think of other good games for a team.
3. Do you think the team should have a teacher or somebody's dad in charge?
4. Why do you think Ginger has no football boots?
5. Do you think Tony should be leader because he thought of the idea, or the best player, or the oldest boy, or who?
6. Is Tony's a good way of deciding? Can you think of any other ways?
7. Find out how a team might join a Junior League.
8. Find out how you book a pitch to play on in the park.
9. Can you think of other things the team might need money for?
10. How do you put money in the bank? How do you put money in the Post Office?
11. Draw a picture or a diagram explaining how a bank or Post Office Savings works.
12. Explain about a 'supporters' club' and about 'raffles'.
13. Why do you think they accept South Street's challenge, even though they are not really ready to start playing as a team?
14. Explain about 'friendly' games.
15. Do you think Tony might have chosen his friends, not the best players?
16. Why do you think it took a long time to pick the team?
17. Explain about 'corners' to somebody who knows nothing about football. Use a diagram or a picture.
18. Why did there seem to be two or three blue shirts to every red?
19. Why do you think Ginger felt especially sad?
20. Explain what Peter meant by 'tighten up at the back'.
21. Try to write a coaching book about how to play football, with diagrams and pictures.
22. Make a list of some things you could learn from books, and some that you can't.
23. What sort of plans does a football manager make?
24. Find out what 'treasurers' do.
25. What sort of orders can a team captain give?
    What sort of orders can a manager give?
    What sort of orders can a referee give?
26. Why were Tony and Ginger only elected for six matches? Was that fair?
27. What sorts of football training could four or five boys do together?

Or one boy on his own?

28. Why is Ginger able to *tell* the Rangers what to do now?
29. Do you agree with Tony or with Peter in the argument about Ginger?
30. Why do you think Tony was so glad about the goal Rangers scored?
31. Make a set of pictures showing Tony showing Rangers the corner-move, Rangers practising it, and Alan scoring the goal in the real game.
32. Why are 'away' games harder?
33. Why did Rangers forget the moves they had been practising?
34. Why did Peter shout more and more?
35. Why do you think it got easier after Tony scored the goal?
36. Find out when and how your local league team started.
37. How do League teams get money, and what do they spend it on?
38. Who is the manager of your local team?
39. How do professional footballers train? How often do they train?
40. How do League teams get new players?
41. Do you mind a lot if your local team loses? Some people mind a lot — why, do you think?
42. How do football pools work? Who gets the money? Why do people do the pools?

Tasks — B (for less able children)

1. Would you like to play football in a proper team? Would it be better than just playing with your friends?
2. Think of a good name for a football team.
3. Think of two things you would have to buy if you were going to play football in a proper team?
4. What does the *captain* of a football team do?
5. Look at the list of things they had to decide (page 201). Can you think of one more thing?
6. Find out what a *League* is.
7. Make a list of things you spend your money on. What things do you save up to buy?
8. How many ways of saving money can you think of?
9. What does it mean if somebody gives a 'challenge'?
10. What do *forwards* do in a team?
11. Find out what a 'treasurer' does.
12. Why were Tony and Peter chosen for only six matches?

13. Make up some of the sums about money that Ginger might have to do.
14. Think of as many things as you can that you could do to get better at football. Could you learn any of them from a book?
15. Make a list of all the people who can tell you what to do.
16. Say in your own words what an 'away' match is.
17. Say in your own words what the 'First Division' is.
18. Find out when your local team started.
19. Who is the manager of your local team?
20. How do League teams get new players?
21. Do you mind a lot if your local team loses?
    Some people mind a lot — why, do you think?

The Teacher's Own Knowledge

As in the case of 'Red Indians', the teacher needs to know enough about our exemplary topic, Victorian England, to make informal planning decisions. The information required is not esoteric and might neatly be summed up as adequate knowledge of the six areas listed on page 211, beginning with '. . . kind of homes people lived in'.

Topics on Finding out about the Past

One aspect of topic work in the junior school will be the study of groups of people who lived in a different time from the present. These may be groups in the recent past such as may be considered in topics that consider life in Grandma's days, or rather more distant groups such as the Victorians or groups in the much more remote past such as the Vikings or Stone Age man. It is also of course likely that a great many topics undertaken will quite naturally be able to develop a consideration of the past as compared with the present and so on. For example topics on 'transport', 'my family', 'people who help us', 'our school', 'towns and villages' could all usefully spend some time looking at the way the evidence they use was collected. This in turn requires some investigation into the situation as it was.

The historical aspect of junior school topic work is then likely to be very significant in terms of the amount of time that is likely to be given to it as either an input into a general topic or a specific study of some historical period or group from historical time. Most junior school teachers will already be aware that the approach to the historical aspects of topic work with young children is not one that is preoccupied with chronology — reigns, periods and dates. Whatever the justifications that may be put forward at the secondary school stage and later, for certain quite specific historical content to be introduced into the curriculum, it seems to us that at the junior school stage the study of history as part of topic work ought to have four main concerns.

The first is to illustrate the notion that neither the present nor the past is unique or static. The present has almost always been influenced by the past. This means that it is not enough to describe the present as it is or the past as it was and leave it at that. The similarities and differences between past and present and between one period in history and another need to be teased out in order to provide opportunities for the relationships between them to be analysed and understood.

It follows from this that understanding change and knowing about change is an essential condition for understanding the world as it is today. It means knowing not only that change is the central concern of historical studies for junior school children but for their understanding of the present, too. Change is going on all the time and so is something children in school should get to know about. A topic on 'homes' or 'transport' or 'the Victorians' should not be presented as aspects of life in a static form, but in terms of the changes that have taken place in relation to these things, the seeking of reasons for these changes and some evaluation of how these changes have affected both the past and the present and the people within them.

The third concern is one that is central to the contentions about topic work being made in this book. We have stressed throughout that information learning is largely merely incidental to the main learning of concepts and skills. The central conceptual development that history provides for at this stage is very commonly within the context of social and political change and its causes and effects. But history also has a process of thinking which, as it is learned, develops intellectual strategies or skills and so contributes significantly to general intellectual development. The idea that the past and the present are interrelated depends in turn for its development on the idea of 'evidence'. The search for appropriate evidence is part of the process of enquiry. This means that such work in topics will involve getting children to collect evidence, getting them to interpret and explain the evidence and, perhaps most importantly, getting them to be a little cynical about the evidence they collect and to appreciate that sometimes evidence is far from complete, is sometimes conflicting and is, at best, unless very recent and available at first hand, to be regarded as tentative. Topic work which does not include an enquiry approach of this kind where evidence is translated, interpreted, evaluated, etc., is unlikely to develop as such, as it might, the ability in children to form reasoned judgements and conclusions — a central aim of education as a whole.

Finally, junior school history — indeed history as a subject — is about people. It is concerned with what they did and the reasons they did it. It is also concerned with the effects that the decisions and behaviour of some people had on other people and how each group felt about the other groups and their behaviour. In almost every case people have choices about how they behave, what decisions they take, how they treat other people. The choice they make will depend upon the particular set of values they hold. People who value material possessions will make choices which are likely to be different from people who value such things as democracy or freedom of speech. Children ought to be given opportunities to understand the differing kinds of values people hold, and how these affect the choices people make and, in turn, the kind of social groups that exist.

Let us take Victorian England as an example of a mainly historical topic. Such a topic would enable us to develop the fundamental idea that society is in a constant state of change. If we think of the attributes of the concept of change and group these attributes in order of difficulty and abstractions we might come up with three stages in the understanding of that idea as we would want to develop it with children in the context of this topic.

The first stage would be simply getting children to realise that change is when something is different from before. In the context of the Victorians this would mean the children being able to identify and describe differences between Victorian society and society at other periods — including the present.

The second stage would be concerned with the understanding that changes have causes. Here the topic would provide opportunities for children to identify the specific reasons for specific changes. Such reasons would include the application of new knowledge, the effects of discoveries and inventions and the development of different values.

Thirdly, an understanding of social change would need to include some ability to evaluate the effects on society generally and on groups or individuals within it. Some people benefit from change, others do not. At any rate people have had different opinions about the effects of change. Frequently minority groups have suffered because of changes which have been of benefit to the majority. But a major concern here is to relate change to such things as increased efficiency and possible economic advantages, to increased opportunity, to better or worse living conditions, to more tolerant attitudes and greater or less equality.

These attributes can form then, the basis for a study of Victorian England which can be used not only to develop an understanding of the concept itself and the generalisation about changing society, but also a range of other concepts such as similarity, difference, minority, majority, values, knowledge, inventions and technology.

To develop these understandings through the topic we would need to provide a range of information about aspects of life in Victorian times. We will need to provide evidence of such things as:

— the kind of homes people lived in
— the kind of work they did
— the degree to which industry was mechanised
— the way the Victorians traded and distributed goods
— the extent to which they were able to communicate with other groups
— the attitudes they held about children, women, race, etc.

Children can be actively involved in collecting much of the evidence. Whilst books and pictures will be important resources, it will also be possible to look at maps of the locality drawn at different times noticing, for example, the way in which street names suggest evidence of change as England developed during the industrial revolution and beyond. It might be possible too to look at the older houses in the district of both the 'working' and 'upper' classes of the time, and to begin to identify and analyse the differing values held and the differing effects of change on these two distinct social groups. Graveyards and headstones provide considerable evidence of life-span generally and indications of infant and child mortality and the deaths of women in childbirth. Headstones describing the wife as a relic of the husband might say, too, something about certain values that prevailed at the time. Of course museums abound which have a wealth of industrial and domestic Victoriana. Artefacts of this kind provide the best evidence of things as they were to which things as they are can be compared. The children can be asked to list some of these differences and to categorise them. Their lists will show different ways of doing things, e.g. caring for the sick, offering goods for sale; the use of different materials, e.g. plastic and alloys; different feelings about things, e.g. the employment of children.

These differences, once identified through one form of evidence can be researched further to determine possible reasons for using different materials — easier to clean, lighter, more attractive, does not conduct heat, etc. — and the effects of these changes in terms of efficiency, convenience and the like.

A study of evidence of child or infant mortality would lead towards some categorisation of the causes of death and the prevalence or otherwise of disease and infection in children today. This can be used to develop ideas about the effect of new knowledge and new values on society and to the evaluation of the consequent changes on family, life, the size of families, the role of women in society.

Parish records and census returns might also be a source of useful evidence of changes in population distribution and work categories. Reasoning the relationship between changes in these two matters and the incidence of technological progress and industrial development would, like all the other tasks suggested here, have the effect of making the children use, think about and firmly grasp the ideas involved and, at the same time, draw them towards understanding the generalisation we have focused upon.

The role of the teacher, of course, is not only to provide information but to require children to collect information themselves from a wide variety of sources — books, maps, graphs, pictures, museums, the locality; set a wide variety of activities such as writing, drawing, making graphs and diagrams, making models and acting roles; require the children within the tasks to infer, evaluate, extrapolate, apply knowledge and other thinking processes (such as are described in some detail elsewhere in this book) and generally in the context of the idea of change involve the child in:

(a) finding out what things were like and seek reasons;
(b) detail changes/differences and suggest reasons for this;
(c) evaluate the changes in terms of their effect on people, situations, attitudes, etc.

Of course change is not the only notion that has been developed in looking at change in relation to a specific historical period. We have already listed some of the other important ideas that would be introduced and developed, to which could be added early notions about ideas such as efficiency, labour-saving and economics.

Such important ideas, if the child is to develop his grasp of them, will need to be introduced in other contexts and this can frequently be achieved through historical inputs in topics which are basically about contemporary situations. A topic on 'transport' for example could usefully look at the difference between early and later forms of transport in relation to their relative efficiency and the effect of that efficiency on man's ability to communicate with others. Similarly a topic on 'shops' could look at the development of the supermarket as against the corner shop in terms of such ideas as efficiency and convenience.

History-based topics can of course be used to develop other important ideas besides the notion of social change as a constant aspect of life.

A study of history can provide us with examples of more primitive societies than exist today and which, by virtue of the less sophisticated ideas involved, can be used to illustrate and exemplify initial ideas about such concepts as culture, agriculture, trade and communication as well as helping the understanding of generalisations such as how the environment affects the cultural behaviour of groups in society (the work they do, the houses they build, the clothes they wear, etc.) Stone Age man would be an example of such a primitive society, and our own topic on 'Red Indians' is an extended illustration of another example.

The 'Red Indian' example shows clearly that the evidential aspect of a study set in the past can be either played up or played down, according to the teacher's judgement. The arrival of horse-herds on the Plains of North America in the seventeenth century is taken as a 'given' in the 'Red Indian' topic, partly because attention needs to be focused very clearly on the effects of this event, not on the evidence for it, and not even on the antecedents to the event, i.e. the escape of the original horses from their Spanish owners. Another reason for neglecting the question 'how do we know?' in this case, is that the nature of the evidence does not lend itself too well to junior investigation. In the case of the Norman Conquest, though, we have the Bayeux Tapestry, an immensely interesting and, literally, colourful example of 'how we know', and it would be missing a great opportunity *not* to make the concept of 'evidence' one of our targets in such a case. Almost any topic can have a 'historical background' input and/or a 'how do we know all this' slant, if we so choose. Whether we so choose will depend on the nature of the accessible evidence, and on the way we order our priorities.

FURTHER READING

1. Concepts

Blank, M. *Teaching Learning in the Pre-School: a Dialogue Approach*, Merrill, 1973
  This book, concerned with conceptual development in young children, suggests strategies which can be applied to rather older children.

Bruner, J. *The Process of Education*, Harvard, 1962

Bruner, J. *Towards a Theory of Instruction*, Harvard, 1966
  Jerome Bruner's curriculum development project, *Man, a Course of Study*, is not available for purchase through booksellers, because its author intended that it should only be used by teachers after a rigorous programme of training. It has been introduced into groups of English schools by some local education authorities and the Centre for Applied Research at the University of East Anglia, Norwich is responsible for its diffusion in this country.

Coltham, J.B. *The Development of Thinking and the Learning of History*, Historical Association, 1971
  While this pamphlet is not concerned exclusively with primary school children it illuminates the problems of conceptual development very helpfully.

Elliott, G. *Teaching for Concepts*, Collins, 1976
  This is a small handbook produced in connection with *Place, Time and Society*, the Schools Council project which identified key concepts in history, geography and the social sciences to be cultivated with children 8-13.

Gunning, S. and D. 'Concepts and Thinking Skills: Teaching Strategies in History and Social Studies', *Education* 3-13, vol. 4, no. 1, April 1976, pp. 43-7

Morrisett, I. (ed.) *Concepts and Structure in the New Social Studies*, Holt, Rinehart and Wilson, 1967
  If you are interested in finding out the 'structure' of say geography, you might consult this book to find out what some geographers think about the matter.

Taba, H. *et al. A Teacher's Handbook to Elementary Social Studies*, Addison Wesley, 1971
  This is a mine of helpful suggestions and useful strategies for teachers

and deserves to be known more widely. It is followed by a series of six books which give a teaching programme for children from six to twelve years old. Although it is directed to American schools and refers to books and materials not available in England, it contains lesson plans on such topics as families and the supermarket which could be adapted by teachers to their own purposes and situation. Hilda Taba's overall philosophy has been strongly influenced by Jerome Bruner's ideas on curriculum development.

Wann, K.D. *Fostering Intellectual Development in Young Children*, Teachers' College Press, 1962
Although this book gives only a brief section on social studies and is concerned with pre-school children, it gives some helpful illustrations of how the foundations of conceptual development can be laid.

Skills

Beck, C.M. (ed.) *Moral Education: Interdisciplinary Approaches*, Toronto University Press, 1971
See especially Kohlberg, L., 'Stages in Moral Development as a Basis for Moral Education', pp. 23-92
Blank, M. & Solomon, F. 'A Tutorial Language Programme to Develop Abstract Thinking in Socially Disadvantaged Pre-school Children', *Child Development*, 39, 1968, pp. 379-89
Bloom, B.S. *et al. Taxonomy of Educational Objectives*, Longmans, 1965
This important work not only lists the intellectual skills but gives examples of tasks invoking them taken from many disciplines. The examples however are not directly helpful to the teachers of young children since the majority of the illustrations are drawn from secondary and higher education.
Bono, de E. *Children Solve Problems*, Penguin, 1972
Bono, de E. *Teaching Thinking*, Smith, 1976
In this book de Bono not only elaborates his position on teaching children to think but reports on his personal curriculum development project CORT, published by the Cognitive Research Trust, Cambridge.
Coltham, J.B. & Fines, J. *Educational Objectives for the Study of History*, Historical Association, 1971
This represents a valuable attempt to adapt Bloom's taxonomy to the purposes of one discipline, history.

Miscellaneous

Barnes, D. *Language, the Learner and the School*, Penguin, 1969

We are indebted to Douglas Barnes for the opportunity to study examples of discussions held by small groups of eleven-year-old children on academic topics in school.

Donaldson, M. *Children's Minds*, Fontana, 1978

Heater, D.B. *The Teaching of Politics*, Methuen, 1969
This book contains a useful chapter by William Gardner summarising what is known about children's political socialisation and refers the reader to further books on that subject.

Herman, W.L. *Current Research in Elementary Social Studies*, Macmillan, 1969

Tough, J. *Focus on Meaning*, Unwin, 1973

2. Social Studies

Blyth, A. *et al. Place Time and Society 8-13*, Collins, 1976
This project, covering the disciplines history, geography and the social sciences, tackles the difficult task of identifying key concepts of the disciplines and then cultivating them through appropriate curricular materials. It is accompanied by a series of handbooks, including:

Elliott, G. *Teaching for Concepts*, Collins, 1976

Elliott, G. *Games and Simulations in the Classroom*, Collins, 1976

Cooper, K. *Evaluation, Assessment and Record-keeping in the Classroom*, Collins, 1976

Derricott, R. *et al. Themes in Outline*, Collins, 1977

Lawton, D. *et al. Social Studies 8-13 Schools Council Working Paper 39*, Methuen, 1971
This boldly suggests a complete programme of work for middle school children which progresses in complexity as the children mature and which is sufficiently flexible to allow the teacher to make curricular decisions within the framework provided. For teachers who are not free or are reluctant to commit themselves to the whole scheme, it provides valuable suggestions for social studies topics together with an analysis of what is to be learned.

Taba, H. *et al. The Taba Social Studies Curriculum*, Addison & Wesley, 1969

Science

The Schools Council project *Science 5/13* is extensive and very valuable. Some of the volumes published are likely to be useful to teachers in areas other than science, for example:

Radford, R. *Science from Toys*, Macdonald, 1972
Richard, R. *Time*, Maddonald, 1972

The Schools Council *Progress in Learning Science* project has also tackled the difficult field of children's attitudes and attitude formation e.g. in *Match and Mismatch. Raising Questions*, Oliver & Boyd, 1977 and *Finding Answers*, Oliver & Boyd, 1977.

The following articles describe innovatory history teaching in the primary school involving the introduction of children to the use of records or artefacts as evidence. They are written by people committed to this approach but they illustrate some of the difficulties as well as the strengths of this method.

Blyth, J.E., Young Children and the Past, *Teaching History*, no. 21, June, 1978, pp. 15-19
Holmes, V., A Teaching Kit on Working Children, *Teaching History* vol. III no. 12, Nov. 1974, pp. 297-303
Purkins, S., An Experiment in Family History with First Year Juniors, *Teaching History* Vol. IV, no. 5, May 1976, pp. 250-6
Wheeler, R. & S., History in the Cupboard, *Teaching History* Vol. II, no. 6, Nov. 1971, pp. 117-23

Curriculum Development Projects

Environmental Studies
Harris, M. (ed.) *The Schools Council Environmental Studies Project*, Rupert Hart Davis, 1972
Harris, M. (ed.) *Teacher's Guide: Starting from Maps, Environmental Studies 5-13, Schools Council Working Paper 48, The use of historical resources*, Methuen, 1973
Crosland, R.W. & Moore, S.F.D. *Environmental Studies 5-13. An Evaluation*, Macmillan, 1967-71
Kefford, C.W. *A Programmed Approach to Environmental Studies. A Guide to Programmes 1-12*, Blandford, 1970
Perry, G.S., Jones, E., & Hammersley, A.H., *Teachers' Handbook for Environmental Studies*, Blandford, 1968
On teaching local history in primary schools teachers might also consult articles in *Teaching History*, e.g.:
Wheeler, S. 'Young Children, Documents and the Locality', *Teaching History*, Vol. 1, pp. 181-7

INDEX